THE GREAT
VOYAGER
ADVENTURE

A GUIDED TOUR THROUGH
THE SOLAR SYSTEM

 JULIAN MESSNER

Alan Harris and Paul Weissman

Library of Congress Cataloging-in-Publication Data

Harris, Alan W., 1944 –
  The great Voyager adventure / Alan Harris and Paul Weissman.
     p. cm.
  Includes bibliographical references and index.
  Summary: Discusses the Voyager space probes and the information they have brought back about Jupiter, Saturn, Uranus, and Neptune.
     1. Project Voyager— Juvenile literature. [1. Project Voyager. 2. Planets—Exploration. 3. Outer space—Exploration.] I. Weissman, Paul Robert, 1947–   . II. Title.
  TL789.8.U6V526 1990
  523.4—dc20   90-6423
  ISBN 0-671-72538-6 (LSB)   CIP
  ISBN 0-671-72539-4   AC

Published by Julian Messner, a division of Simon & Schuster, Inc., Prentice Hall Bldg., Englewood Cliffs, NJ 07632.

Produced by: RGA PUBLISHING GROUP, INC.

Project Editors: LISA MELTON AND EMILY EASTON

Design: MIKE YAZZOLINO

Cover design: GIL HUNG

Illustrations: JAMES STAUNTON

Manufactured in the United States of America
10 9 8 7 6 5 4 3 2 1

Acknowledgments

The Voyager mission was a marvelous achievement of science, technology, and exploration. Working at JPL, we were privileged to be able to watch it grow from the drawing board to reality, and then to be there as the spacecraft sent back their incredible photographs and scientific data. We were also privileged to know and work with many of the fine scientists and engineers whose tireless dedication to their task made Voyager a success. We would be remiss if we did not acknowledge the tremendous contribution all these people have made to planetary and space science and to humanity itself. They have pushed the limits of exploration to the edge of the solar system and beyond. This book is about their accomplishments.

We wish to thank the many members of the Voyager flight team who were generous with their time in answering our questions during the writing of this book. We especially wish to thank Linda Horn for reading a draft of the completed text and giving us her valuable comments.

Finally, we wish to thank our editor, Lisa Melton, for putting up with two troublesome scientists who rarely turned their assignments in on time and always seemed to be either busy or traveling or both. This book is as much a product of her efforts as it is ours.

For Catherine
                                  —A.W.H.
For Jason, Andra, Daniel, and Diana —future explorers all.
                                  —P.R.W.

CONTENTS

How to read the timeline

1 ■ *3/4/79 Ring-plane crossing, 11:50 a.m., 744,000 miles (1.2 million km)*

2

1 = **Voyager 1**

2 = **Voyager 2**

3/4/79	**encounter date**
Ring-plane crossing	**event**
11:50 a.m.	**time** signals reached Earth
744,000 miles (1.2 million km)	**distance** of Voyager from object encountered (in both miles and kilometers [km])

Voyager 1 Jupiter Encounter

Light travel time = 38 minutes
Time is Pacific Standard Time

Voyager 2 Jupiter Encounter

Light travel time = 52 minutes
Time is Pacific Daylight Time

Voyager 1 Saturn Encounter

Light travel time = 1 hour 25 minutes
Time is Pacific Standard Time

Voyager 2 Saturn Encounter

Light travel time = 1 hour 27 minutes
Time is Pacific Daylight Time

Voyager 2 Uranus Encounter

Light travel time = 2 hours 45 minutes
Time is Pacific Standard Time

Voyager 2 Neptune Encounter

Light travel time = 4 hours 5 minutes
Time is Pacific Daylight Time

1
2 ■ 1969 *NASA proposes a mission to explore the outer solar system.*

A GRAND TOUR OF THE SOLAR SYSTEM

In 1972, the American space program, under the direction of the National Aeronautics and Space Administration (NASA), was in full swing. Men on the Apollo mission were exploring the Moon. One of the Mariner spacecraft had flown past Venus and another was in orbit around Mars. NASA already had plans to send another Mariner past Venus and on to Mercury, and plans for the Viking missions to orbit and land space vehicles on Mars in time for the United States bicentennial (two-hundredth anniversary) in 1976 were under way.

Also, two probes (Pioneer 10 and Pioneer 11) were scheduled to be launched to fly by the huge planet Jupiter. But compared to the large Mariner and Viking robots exploring the inner planets, these probes were small and simple, and there were no plans to explore anything beyond Jupiter.

A FORTUNATE ALIGNMENT

In the early 1960s, scientists had realized that in the late 1970s a certain alignment of the planets would make it possible for a single spacecraft to fly by all four of the giant planets—Jupiter, Saturn, Uranus, and Neptune—by using the power of each planet's gravity to aim and speed the spacecraft on toward its next encounter. Because these planets orbit the Sun at different rates, such a fortunate alignment occurs only once every 175 years!

It was a remarkable coincidence that another chance to fly by these planets should come in the 1970s, when humankind had just enough technical capability to do the job. Fortunately, the opportunity was seized, and in late 1972 the president and Congress gave NASA the go-ahead to design and build two robotic spacecraft to explore the outer planets. The Voyager mission was born.

The Jet Propulsion Laboratory, Pasadena, California.

The last opportunity to fly by all four of the giant planets occurred during the presidency of Thomas Jefferson. No doubt Mr. Jefferson, who "launched" the Lewis and Clark expedition to explore the central and northwestern United States, would have loved the chance to explore all four of the giant planets.

The scientists at NASA did not get all they wanted, unfortunately. Because of the mission's huge cost, Congress authorized NASA to fly the two spacecraft to only Jupiter and Saturn. Even though the critical launch date (coinciding with the alignment of the planets) was kept, in case it became possible to fly on to Uranus and Neptune, scientists were allowed to include in the spacecraft design only those features that were specifically required for the first two encounters.

But we know that the second space probe launched — Voyager 2 — *did* eventually encounter Uranus and Neptune, even though it hadn't been designed to do that job. How was this done? In the pages that follow you'll learn how the efforts of many hundreds of people working together made the Voyager mission a success. Engineers and scientists spent years designing the spacecraft and all its scientific instruments, and planning out the mission to the tiniest detail. Dozens of

7/1/72 *The Voyager mission officially begins.*

companies all over the United States built individual parts that were assembled into the two Voyager spacecraft at the Jet Propulsion Laboratory (JPL), in Pasadena, California. And once the two spacecraft were assembled, the work of the scientists and engineers was not over. If building the Voyagers was challenging, operating them by remote control over billions of miles for many years was an even trickier task.

The Voyager mission depended on the work of many dedicated individuals whose one common goal was to explore our solar system. In the end, it turned out to be the most successful space mission ever, teaching us that our solar system is a more complex and fascinating place than we had ever imagined.

PLANNING THE TRIP

Sending the two Voyager spacecraft from the Earth to Jupiter to Saturn to Uranus to Neptune was not easy. The scientists and engineers had to carefully plan every phase of the mission months, or even years, in advance. They had to know precisely when each spacecraft would encounter each planet, as well as where each of that planet's moons would be in their orbits at that time.

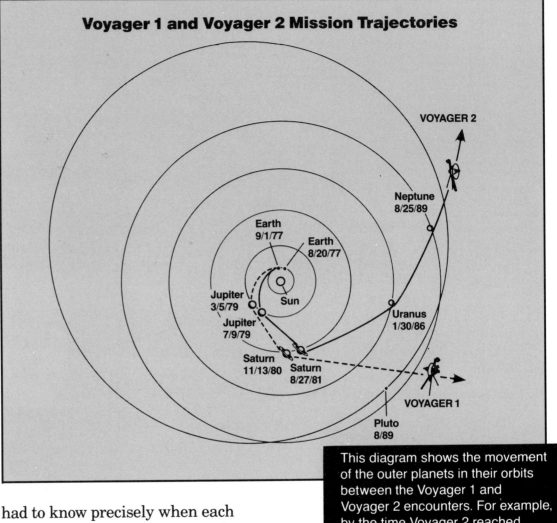

Voyager 1 and Voyager 2 Mission Trajectories

VOYAGER 2

Neptune
8/25/89

Earth
9/1/77

Earth
8/20/77

Jupiter
3/5/79

Sun

Uranus
1/30/86

Jupiter
7/9/79

Saturn
11/13/80

Saturn
8/27/81

VOYAGER 1

Pluto
8/89

This diagram shows the movement of the outer planets in their orbits between the Voyager 1 and Voyager 2 encounters. For example, by the time Voyager 2 reached Jupiter, four months after the Voyager 1 Jupiter encounter, the huge planet had moved many millions of miles in its orbit.

8

12/72 *The Voyager scientists meet at JPL for the first time.*

Because the planets move all the time, the engineers couldn't just aim Voyager at Jupiter and hope to reach it. Instead, they aimed Voyager at where Jupiter would be when the spacecraft got there, just as a football quarterback throws the ball to where a receiver will be when the ball comes down. Fortunately, because scientists have been observing the planets and their satellites for about 300 years, it was possible to predict their positions to within about 100 miles.

Each Voyager needed the gravity from one planet to send it on to the next planet. If the spacecraft missed its aim point at each planet by too many miles, its path would be bent either too much or too little, and it would not get to the next planet. So just before each planetary encounter, the engineers fired Voyager's small rockets to put it on just the right path past that planet to get to the next one. And in case Voyager didn't get just the right push from each planet, another rocket maneuver after each flyby corrected any small error.

How well did the plan work? Well, at Neptune, after traveling for 5 billion miles, Voyager 2 missed its aim point by only 19 miles. That's about the same as a baseball pitcher hitting the strike zone at home plate from a distance of 100,000 miles away!

As Voyager cruised between the planets, the scientists and engineers were still hard at work. They had to analyze all the pictures and data from each encounter and write up the results for others to read. Then they had to plan the next encounter. They also kept thinking of ways to improve each spacecraft by writing more complex computer programs to run the various systems.

Each Voyager was tracked using radio signals. A signal would be sent from Earth, and when the spacecraft received the signal, it would send the signal back. By timing how long it took for the signal to get to Voyager and back, the engineers could figure out how far away the spacecraft was. By measuring the change in the frequency of the signal, they could tell how fast Voyager was moving. Putting many such measurements together, the engineers could figure out Voyager's position in the solar system to within about 30 feet!

A note on speed: Voyager 2 picked up 22,000 miles per hour (relative to the Sun) in its swing past Jupiter. This doubled its speed! It also meant that Voyager 2 would be able to escape the Sun's gravity and exit the solar system. At Saturn, it gained 11,000 miles per hour, and at Uranus, 5,000 miles per hour. At Neptune, it actually lost 7,000 miles per hour, but this was not enough to stop its flight out of the solar system. (Roughly the same figures apply for Voyager 1's encounters with Jupiter and Saturn.)

A LOOK AT OUR SOLAR SYSTEM

Our Sun is a star, just like the distant points of light you see in the night sky. On a really clear night, far from city lights and smog, you can see about 2,000 stars. But there are billions more out there. Our solar system is part of the Milky Way galaxy, which alone contains 100 million stars, and our galaxy is only one of millions of galaxies in the universe. Our Sun is an average star, not very bright and not very faint. But because we live close to it, it gives us the light and heat that make life on Earth possible.

The Earth is one of nine planets that orbit the Sun. Each planet is very different from its neighbor. Some differences are caused by each planet's distance from the Sun; the closer planets, for example, receive much more light and heat from the Sun than do the more distant planets. Other differences are caused by what the planets are made of or by the different events that have happened to each of them over their histories.

10

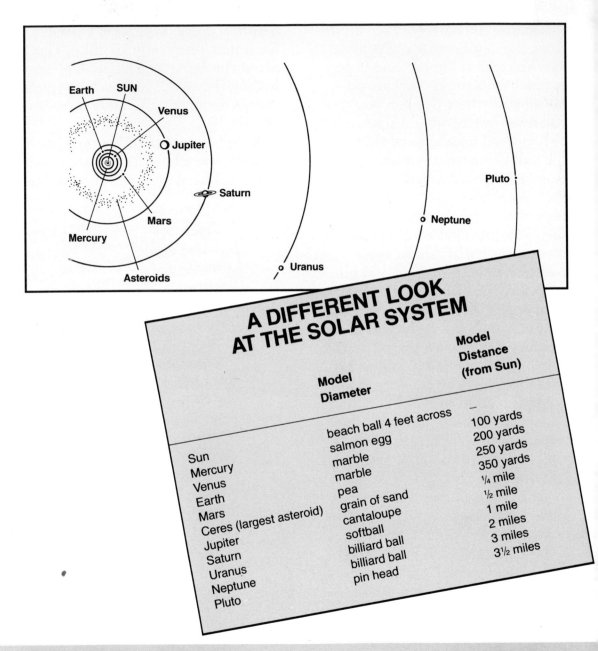

A DIFFERENT LOOK AT THE SOLAR SYSTEM

	Model Diameter	Model Distance (from Sun)
Sun	beach ball 4 feet across	
Mercury	salmon egg	100 yards
Venus	marble	200 yards
Earth	marble	250 yards
Mars	pea	350 yards
Ceres (largest asteroid)	grain of sand	¼ mile
Jupiter	cantaloupe	½ mile
Saturn	softball	1 mile
Uranus	billiard ball	2 miles
Neptune	billiard ball	3 miles
Pluto	pin head	3½ miles

Mercury

Venus

Mars

Earth

The two innermost planets, Mercury and Venus, were photographed by Mariner 10 in 1974 and 1975. The picture of the Earth was taken from space by Apollo astronauts on their way back from the Moon, and the picture of Mars was taken by Viking in 1976.

Saturn

The pictures of Jupiter, Saturn, Uranus, and Neptune were taken from the Earth and are as good as any we had before the Voyager mission.

Jupiter

Uranus

Neptune

9/18/77 *Voyager 1 takes a photograph of the Earth and Moon in crescent.*

Scientists have calculated the sizes of all the planets and their distances from the Sun. (These figures, as well as figures for the moons of each planetary system Voyager encountered, are provided at the back of this book.) The table shown here offers an alternate view of the solar system and what it would look like were a scale model to be made of it. Similar tables for Jupiter, Saturn, Uranus, and Neptune are also provided.

The planets closest to the Sun are Mercury, Venus, Earth, and Mars. These planets are all made of rock. Mercury is about three times closer to the Sun than the Earth and is so hot that its atmosphere has boiled away. Its surface is covered with craters, much like our own Moon. Venus is halfway between Mercury and the Earth and is also extremely hot. Its atmosphere is 95 times thicker than the Earth's, and its surface is covered by volcanos spewing hot lava. Mars, which is about one-and-a-half times further from the Sun than the Earth, is colder and has less than 1/100th as much air at the surface. Much of the Martian surface is covered with craters.

Voyager visited the solar system's giant outer planets. These are Jupiter, Saturn, Uranus, and Neptune. Instead of being made of rock, these planets are made mostly of gas. Jupiter and Saturn are composed mostly of hydrogen and helium, the same gases that make up the Sun. Uranus and Neptune also contain some hydrogen and helium but are made mostly of water vapor and methane and ammonia gases. Because the solar system contained more gas at the time these four planets formed, they are much bigger than the inner planets.

Beyond Neptune is the ninth planet, Pluto. A small body of rock and ice, Pluto is not much bigger than the moons around some of the other outer planets. Pluto has its own moon, a small icy body called Charon (KAR-un).

Are there other planets beyond Pluto? We don't know. Astronomers have searched for other planets for many years, but none has ever been found. Still, the search continues, and someday another may be found.

On these pages are pictures of all of the planets except Pluto. (The "best" picture of Pluto we have is just a dot!) The best pictures of the inner planets were taken from space and are better than any taken from the Earth. The pictures of the four giant planets were taken from the Earth. Compare them to what follows!

At the beginning of the Voyager mission, scientists had an important decision to make. One of the two spacecraft (it was hoped) would be visiting Jupiter, Saturn, Uranus, and Neptune, but the other could visit *either* the very interesting satellite Titan, at Saturn, *or* Pluto (by using gravity assists from Jupiter and Saturn). The spacecraft could not do both, since a close approach to Titan would fling the spacecraft on the wrong trajectory to reach Pluto. The scientists chose Titan.

1 ■ 11/77 *Voyager 1 crosses the orbit of Mars on its way to Jupiter.*

2 ■ 11/77 *Voyager 2 crosses the orbit of Mars on its way to Jupiter.*

THE VOYAGER SPACECRAFT

THE INCREDIBLE MACHINE

Engineers at the Jet Propulsion Laboratory had been designing and building NASA spacecraft for years, but designing the Voyager spacecraft and then building two of them was a new challenge for the engineers. Voyager 1 and Voyager 2 would have to work perfectly in space for years without breaking down. They would have to be able to travel far from the Sun and yet have enough electric power to run all the scientific instruments, computers, radios, and other equipment on board. The Voyagers would also have to send pictures and other information back to Earth, billions of miles away.

The design the engineers came up with satisfied all these requirements. To communicate with the Earth, each spacecraft had 2 **radio transmitters**, 2 **receivers**, and a large **antenna**, 12½ feet across. Below the antenna was a collection of ten boxes arranged in a circle; these were called the **spacecraft bus.** Each of the boxes held different parts of the spacecraft: the radio transmitters and receivers, the tape recorder, and the computers. Placing all the boxes

■ 12/77 *Voyager 1 enters the asteroid belt.*

■ 12/77 *Voyager 2 enters the asteroid belt.*

together made it easier to keep the electronics warm in the cold of deep space.

One of the biggest problems that had to be solved was where each Voyager would get the electricity to run all of its instruments. Earlier spacecraft had used solar cells, which convert sunlight directly into electricity. But the Voyagers were going so far from the Sun that the sunlight would be too weak. It was decided that instead of solar cells, the Voyagers would use **radioisotope thermoelectric generators (RTGs).** The generators used a fuel called plutonium, a radioactive element that decays over time. When plutonium decays, it releases heat. The Voyager generators changed the heat into the needed electricity.

When the generators on each Voyager were brand-new, they could generate about 450 watts of electricity. Is that a lot? Well, an ordinary light bulb uses about 100 watts, so each Voyager spacecraft had enough energy to run about four and a half light bulbs—not very much, when you think about it! Voyager 1 and Voyager 2 each had to run 11 scientific instruments, 3 computers, a tape recorder, 2 different radio transmitters, and other equipment. At the same time, each spacecraft had to run heaters to keep everything close to room temperature.

The RTGs on Voyager were mounted on a **boom,** a metal arm that extended out from the side of the spacecraft bus. The boom was folded down to fit inside a rocket nose cone during launch. When Voyager entered outer space, the boom was opened by springs and explosive bolts.

Opposite the bus was another boom that carried most of the scientific instruments. This "science boom" also folded down for launch. At the end of the boom was a steerable platform called the **scan platform.** Mounted on the scan platform were two television **cameras,** one wide angle and the other telephoto. Next to the cameras were two special instruments, called **spectrometers,** that could "see" and measure light that we cannot see with our eyes—ultraviolet (UV) and infrared (IR) light. A third instrument, called a **photopolarimeter,** measured exactly how bright the light was.

Another set of instruments on the science boom measured the **solar wind,** the charged particles that flow out from the Sun; the amount of charged particles in orbit around each of the planets the space probes would encounter; and the amount of **cosmic rays,** which are very

14

The Voyager Spacecraft and Scientific Instruments

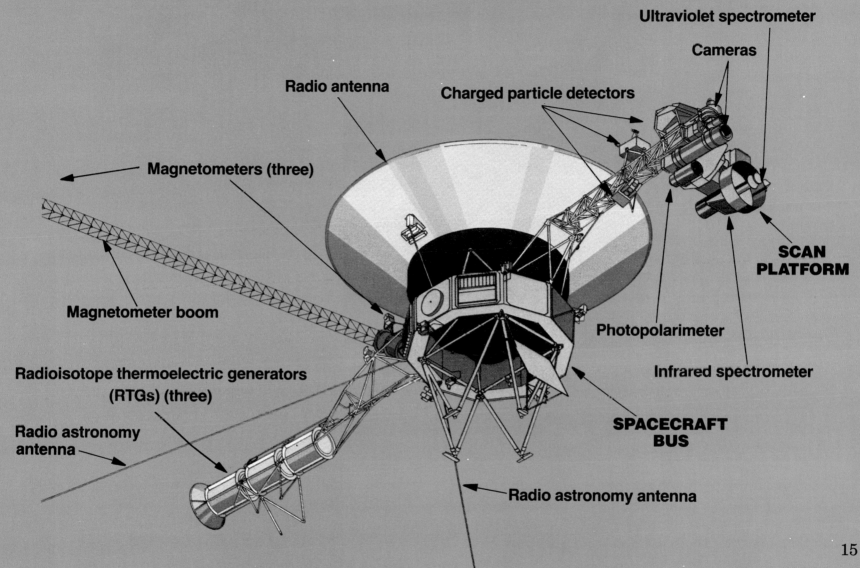

Ultraviolet spectrometer

Cameras

Radio antenna

Charged particle detectors

Magnetometers (three)

Magnetometer boom

SCAN PLATFORM

Photopolarimeter

Radioisotope thermoelectric generators (RTGs) (three)

Infrared spectrometer

Radio astronomy antenna

SPACECRAFT BUS

Radio astronomy antenna

energetic particles that come from beyond the solar system.

A very important instrument on Voyager was the **magnetometer,** which was to measure the magnetic fields of each of the planets. Since each spacecraft itself generated a small magnetic field, the magnetometer had to be mounted as far away from the rest of the spacecraft as possible. The magnetometer was placed at the end of its own 43-foot-long boom; during launch, this boom was folded up like a jack-in-the-box into a canister only about 1 foot long, but in space it was opened up to its full length.

To command the spacecraft, the engineers put three computers on board both Voyagers. One computer kept the spacecraft antenna pointed toward Earth at all times and the cameras and other instruments pointed at each planet and satellite as the spacecraft encountered them. A second computer accepted all the commands that the engineers on Earth continually sent to the Voyagers. This computer also relayed the commands to the different parts of the spacecraft.

Finally, a third computer collected all the pictures and data that the Voyagers gathered and directed them to the radios for transmission back to Earth.

Sometimes the Voyager spacecraft were so busy accumulating pictures and data that the computers couldn't send it all back to Earth at once. When that happened, the computers sent the data to a special tape recorder—something like a VCR—and later played it back when things were less busy.

In addition to all the above, both Voyager 1 and Voyager 2 had 16 small **rocket motors** to help turn and point them and also to help steer them on their way to each planet.

After designing all the instruments, the engineers had to deal with this question: What if, after the Voyagers were millions of miles out in space, an important instrument broke down on one of them? Obviously, there wouldn't be any way to send a repairman out to fix the broken instrument, so engineers decided that the critical parts of the Voyagers should be duplicated. Thus, on each

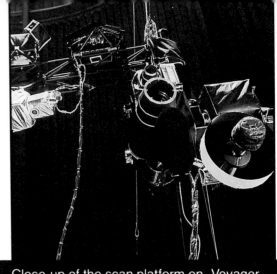

Close-up of the scan platform on Voyager.

spacecraft, each of the three computers had an identical computer just like it, ready to take its place if it broke down. Each radio transmitter and receiver also had a duplicate. Perhaps most important, if one of the Voyagers broke down completely, the other could carry on and complete the mission.

All of this planning turned out to be a good idea, because less than a year after launch one radio receiver on Voyager 2 failed. Without its backup receiver, Voyager 2 would never have made it to Jupiter, much less the more than 4 billion miles more to Neptune.

16

1 ■ **9/78** *Voyager 1 exits the asteroid belt.*

2 ■ **9/78** *Voyager 2 exits the asteroid belt*

THE DEEP SPACE NETWORK

Voyager's radio signals were received on Earth by three huge, dish-shaped, movable radio antennas, each more than 210 feet in diameter. The antennas were located around the world at roughly one-third intervals, so that one antenna would be in position to talk with Voyager at any time. The antennas needed to be in places where it doesn't rain very often, because rain made it difficult to detect the signals from Voyager. Also, the antennas had to be as far as possible from ordinary radio and television stations, which could interfere with the spacecraft's faint signals. One antenna was placed in the Mojave Desert at Goldstone, California; a second was placed in southeastern Australia near the city of Canberra; and the third was placed in Spain, not far from its capital city, Madrid. At each of these locations, two smaller dish antennas (each 112 feet in diameter) were also used to talk with Voyager. Together, these antennas make up

The 210-foot-wide Deep Space Network antenna at Goldstone, California. The diameter of this and the other large DSN antennas was increased to 230 feet for the Neptune encounter.

what NASA calls the **Deep Space Network,** or **DSN.**

Besides listening to Voyager, the antennas were also used to send commands to it, loading the spacecraft's computer memory with instructions on what to do at each planet. But as Voyager got further and further away, its signals became weaker and weaker. So NASA used the three years while Voyager was cruising from Uranus to Neptune to enlarge the big antennas even more, to 230 feet in diameter. NASA also arranged to use other radio antennas around the world—in Japan, Australia, and New Mexico—to help in receiving the faint signals.

17

One of the complete Voyager spacecraft, with its booms folded, undergoes testing in a cleanroom at JPL.

ASSEMBLY AND TESTING

The two Voyager spacecraft were assembled at the Jet Propulsion Laboratory in special rooms called cleanrooms, which are kept even cleaner than hospital operating rooms. Special air conditioners filtered out all the dust particles in the air, and all of the engineers and technicians who worked in the cleanrooms had to wear special suits to prevent any dust on their clothing or hair from falling onto the highly sensitive spacecraft parts. If any dirt got on any one of the thousands of parts on the spacecraft during assembly, it could prevent the Voyager from working perfectly or cause it to wear out over time.

When they were finished, each of the two identical Voyager spacecraft was made up of 65,000 individual parts and weighed 1,815 pounds. The two Voyagers were then tested over and over again to make certain they would work perfectly in space for many years. The computer programs that would run the Voyagers in space were simulated.

The spacecraft were even put in a giant vacuum chamber that could duplicate both the searing heat of the Sun and the bitter cold of outer space.

When they were ready, the Voyagers were driven across the United States to Cape Canaveral, in Florida. There they were hoisted on top of giant Titan III rockets. Engineers had carefully calculated the best day to launch each spacecraft toward Jupiter. The first Voyager was launched on August 20, 1977, but it was named Voyager 2 because it was directed on a longer path to Jupiter. Voyager 1, which was launched on September 5, 1977—16 days after Voyager 2— would reach Jupiter a full four months earlier than its twin.

Once the Voyagers were launched, the scientists and engineers set to work testing those parts of the spacecraft that could only be operated in the weightlessness of outer space. Other parts had to be carefully checked and aligned because the rocket launch gave each Voyager a good shaking, and things might not be exactly the way they

Voyager was placed in the thermal vacuum chamber at JPL to simulate conditions in outer space, far from the Sun.

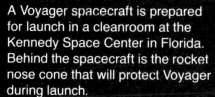

A Voyager spacecraft is prepared for launch in a cleanroom at the Kennedy Space Center in Florida. Behind the spacecraft is the rocket nose cone that will protect Voyager during launch.

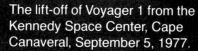

The lift-off of Voyager 1 from the Kennedy Space Center, Cape Canaveral, September 5, 1977.

should be when the spacecraft were put together.

One big problem scientists had to face just after launch was that the spacecraft refused to accept commands from Earth. Each Voyager had been equipped with computer programs that checked commands sent to it to see if the commands were safe to execute. In this way, if a command had become garbled by the time it reached the spacecraft, Voyager would not do the wrong thing and damage itself. However, these computer programs turned out to be *too* cautious, and Voyager refused to execute perfectly good commands. So, the engineers had to figure out where the problem was and rewrite the computer programs. When these new programs were radioed to the Voyagers, they began operating much better.

As the Voyagers cruised toward Jupiter, the engineers and scientists practiced for the Jupiter encounter and made certain that everything would go right. It was a lot of work, but it would have a big payoff when the spacecraft arrived at its first destination.

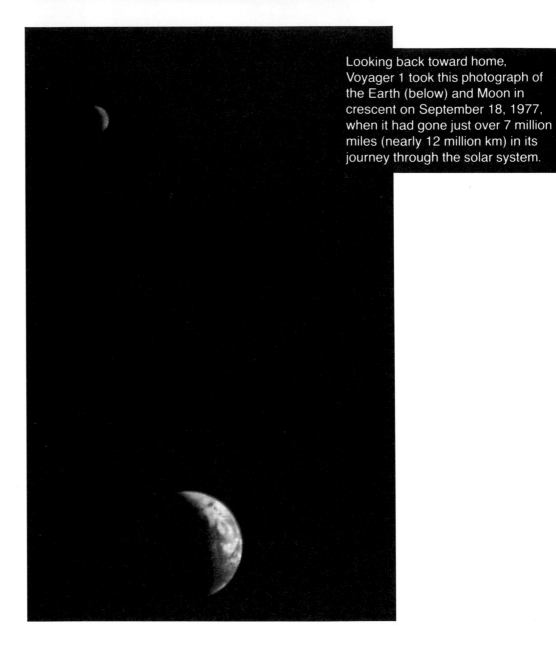

Looking back toward home, Voyager 1 took this photograph of the Earth (below) and Moon in crescent on September 18, 1977, when it had gone just over 7 million miles (nearly 12 million km) in its journey through the solar system.

■ **2/10/79   *Voyager 1 crosses the orbit of Jupiter's outermost satellite, Sinope, 14 million miles (23 million km) from Jupiter. It has now entered the Jovian system.***

JUPITER
THE FIRST ENCOUNTER

The first stop on Voyager's cosmic journey was the giant planet Jupiter. The largest planet in the solar system, Jupiter is 11 times the diameter of the Earth and weighs 300 times as much. You might think that such a giant would rotate more slowly than the Earth, but actually it spins around much faster, making one rotation in less than 10 hours. Jupiter is 5 times farther from the Sun than we are. Its **year**—that is, the time it takes the planet to travel once around the Sun—is almost 12 Earth years.

Jupiter has four large moons, three of which are bigger than the Earth's Moon. These moons, discovered in 1610 by Galileo Galilei, are commonly called the Galilean satellites. Nine smaller moons were also known before the two Voyager flybys.

The Earth and the other planets near it—Mercury, Venus, and Mars—are made of rock. But Jupiter is very different. It is a giant ball of gas, made up mostly of hydrogen and helium. That means it has no solid surface on which you could stand! The thick atmosphere would just become more and more

Scientists measure distance from the Sun in terms of **astronomical units,** or **AU.** The Earth is used to provide the standard—it is 93 million miles (150 million km), or one AU, from the Sun. Jupiter is five AUs from the Sun.

21

The huge planet Jupiter, in one of the first photographs taken by Voyager 1, on January 26, 1979. Even at 29 million miles (47 million km) from the planet, the spacecraft's cameras picked up details of colorful clouds and swirling storm systems. They also spotted Ganymede (right center) and Europa (top right), two of the four Galilean satellites. OPPOSITE: Look carefully and you'll see two of Jupiter's moons — Io (left) and Europa. Voyager 1 took this photograph on February 13, 1979, when it was 12½ million miles (20 million km) from the planet.

dense as you sank deeper into the planet. At the very center of Jupiter is a relatively tiny core of rock and ice — tiny for Jupiter, that is. This core is about the size of the Earth.

Astronomers on Earth have been watching Jupiter through telescopes for centuries. About 300 years ago, they noticed a giant storm raging in the planet's atmosphere. The storm

was big enough to swallow up two Earths. Because the clouds appeared pinkish-red, this storm was called the Great Red Spot. Unlike clouds on Earth, which are made of tiny drops of water and ice, the clouds on Jupiter are made of methane (the same compound as natural gas) and ammonia—a very poisonous, smelly combination!

It took Voyager 1 exactly one and a half years to travel the 500 million miles to Jupiter. On March 5, 1979, it flew within about 172,000 miles (277,400 km) of the planet's cloud tops. But it had been observing Jupiter with its cameras and other instruments for many months, and as it zoomed closer and closer, the pictures of the planet and its

3/5/79 *Amalthea CA (closest approach), 1:40 a.m., 260,400 miles (420,000 km)*

1
2

The Great Red Spot — a huge storm twice the size of Earth — in a mosaic of photos taken by Voyager 2.

23

3/5/79 *Jupiter CA, 4:42 a.m., 172,000 miles (277,400 km)*

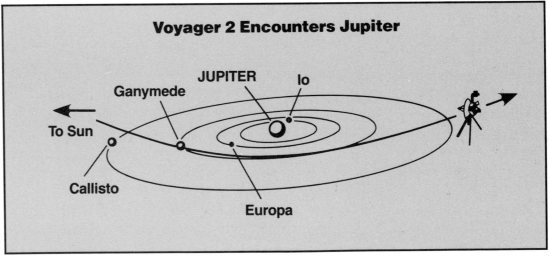

Voyager 1 Encounters Jupiter

JUPITER

Ganymede

To Sun

Callisto

Io

Amalthea

Jupiter's violent atmosphere, as seen from just over 1 million miles (nearly 2 million km) away.

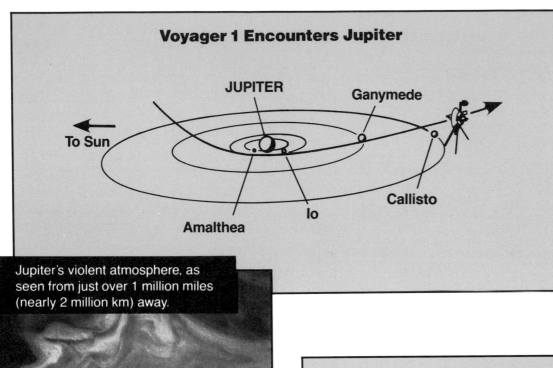

satellites that it sent back to Earth became more and more detailed. In Voyager 1's encounter with Jupiter, its cameras took 18,000 pictures.

What Voyager 1 showed us was a huge planet with a tremendously active atmosphere. Fierce winds blew clouds violently around the planet. The Great Red Spot was still raging, and many other smaller storms, each bigger than the Earth's Moon, were scattered around the planet. Pictures taken by Voyager 1 as it passed the planet showed huge lightning bolts in the clouds and auroras still higher in the upper atmosphere. Jupiter was anything but dull!

Voyager 2 Encounters Jupiter

Ganymede

JUPITER

Io

To Sun

Callisto

Europa

1
2 ■ 3/5/79 *Io CA, 7:47 a.m., 12,750 miles (20,570 km)*

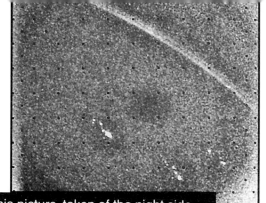

This picture, taken of the night side of Jupiter, shows a large aurora along the edge of the planet and, closer up, many giant bolts of lightning flashing in the clouds.

But, of course, it wasn't just the spacecraft's cameras that were busy. All of Voyager's other instruments were gathering information, too, and beaming it back to Earth at a rate of 115,200 bits (or single units) of information per second. (Even though the signals from Voyager traveled at the speed of light, they took 37 minutes to reach us from such a distance.) The charged-particle detectors measured belts of radiation around Jupiter intense enough to kill a human being in a few hours. Some of Voyager's special electronics were damaged by the fierce radiation, but the spacecraft carried on.

Voyager 2 followed Voyager 1 four months later. On July 9, 1979, it swept by Jupiter at an altitude of 403,000 miles (650,200 km)—not as close as Voyager 1, but still deep within the radiation belts. Voyager 2 took 14,900 pictures. The clouds it found appeared different from those Voyager 1 saw, because the fierce winds had blown the clouds into new formations. But the storm called the Great Red Spot was still churning, as it had for centuries.

VOLCANIC IO

As Voyager 1 closed in on Io (EYE-o), the closest large satellite to Jupiter, its cameras revealed a brightly colored surface, painted by layers of the same sulfur and other compounds found near volcanos and geysers on Earth. Instead of impact craters, which dominate most of the solid surfaces in the solar system, Io was seen to be covered with volcanic features: giant calderas (collapsed volcanos), lava-flow channels, and smooth lava beds. Impact craters, like those on our Moon, give us an idea of how old a surface is. Because

the meteor impacts, or collisions, that cause craters don't happen very often (approximately once every few million years), we know that where there are lots of craters, the surface is very old. Voyager 1 discovered no impact craters on Io, so scientists were able to determine that its surface must be less than a million years old.

Because of the lack of craters, scientists also immediately knew that the volcanic activity on Io was recent. But the most exciting discovery came the weekend following the March 6 encounter. While examining a picture of Io, Linda Morabito, an engineer involved with the spacecraft's navigation, noticed an arc extending beyond the edge of Io. At first, she thought this might be another satellite, but it quickly became clear that it was actually the gas plume of an erupting volcano. Io was an *active* moon! The plume belonged to Io's largest volcano, which the scientists named "Pele" (PAY-lay) after the Hawaiian goddess of volcanos. Also visible in the picture is a second plume, from Loki (LOW-ky), Io's second largest volcano.

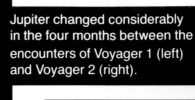

Jupiter changed considerably in the four months between the encounters of Voyager 1 (left) and Voyager 2 (right).

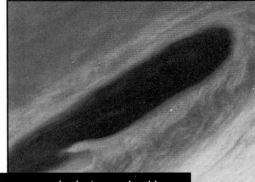

This brown oval, photographed by Voyager 2, is a hole in the high-level ammonia clouds, revealing dark clouds at a lower level. The composition of these lower clouds is not known for sure, but it may be a variety of sulfur and hydrocarbon compounds.

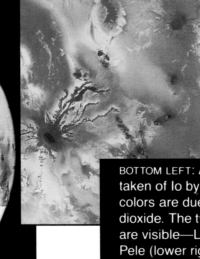

BOTTOM LEFT: A mosaic of pictures taken of Io by Voyager 1. The bright colors are due to sulfur and sulfur dioxide. The two biggest volcanos are visible—Loki (upper left) and Pele (lower right). The blurry band tracing out the heart shape is where the dusty material from the plume lands on Io's surface.

BOTTOM RIGHT: Close-up of the volcanic surface of Io, covering an area about equal to California and Nevada. The surface is covered by volcanic vents and flows, with no trace of impact craters.

26

The navigation photo that revealed the active volcanos. The plume above Pele, the largest volcano, is seen extending out from the edge of Io. The plume from Loki extends from the surface up into the sunlight, just off into the night side of Io.

Tides are caused by the gravitational pull between bodies in orbit around one another. For example, the Moon and the Sun gravitationally pull on the Earth, and as a result of this pulling—or tidal force—the oceans on Earth rise and fall in what we call the tides. Most of the planets and satellites in our solar system are affected by tidal forces, even if they are solid. The energy in the tides turns into heat inside the planet or satellite. On the Earth or Moon, the heating from tides is tiny, but on Io, it is enough to melt large portions of the interior, causing volcanos.

Linda Morabito (above) and the photo she used to discover the volcanic eruptions on Io. The plume above Pele, the largest volcano, is seen extending out from the edge of Io. The plume from Loki extends from the surface up into the sunlight, just off into the night side of Io.

A color-enhanced view of the plume from Loki on the horizon of Io.

27

■ 3/6/79 *Callisto CA, 9:50 a.m., 78,365 miles (126,400 km)*

■ 4/24/79 *Voyager 2 begins its "Observatory Phase," photographing Jupiter.*

Shown side by side: the four large Galilean satellites of Jupiter, as seen by Voyager 1. Io (upper left) and Europa (upper right) are about the size of our Moon. Ganymede (lower left) and Callisto (lower right) are close to the size of the planet Mercury.

Altogether, eight active volcanos were identified from Voyager 1 pictures. Where does the energy for these erupting volcanos come from? The answer is, tides. Io makes two trips around Jupiter for every one trip made by Europa, the next satellite out from Jupiter. The tugging between the two satellites as they pass each other, always in the same place in their orbits, causes their orbits to become eccentric, or egg-shaped. The tidal force from Jupiter tries to pull the orbits back into circles. This pulling releases energy into the satellites, heating them up. In Io, the heating is so great that it causes volcanos.

Now that the scientists knew about Io's volcanos, they could command Voyager 2 to take a closer look when it arrived on the scene. Of the eight known volcanos, Voyager 2 was able to examine seven, and it found all but the first and biggest one, Pele, to be still erupting. So it seems that almost all of the volcanos on Io, unlike those on the Earth, are erupting most of the time, or at least for longer than four months at a time.

OTHER GALILEAN SATELLITES

The two Voyagers mapped all four of Jupiter's largest moons, the so-called Galilean satellites—Io, Europa (yoo-ROH-puh), Ganymede (GAN-uh-meed), and Callisto (kuh-LIS-toh). Ganymede is the largest satellite in the solar system.

Voyager 2 obtained a much better view of Europa, as seen in this close-up view taken from 150,000 miles (240,000 km) away. Details show a crust of ice crossed by long cracks.

Each of the Galilean moons has its own distinct features. Io and Europa are made up mostly of rock. Io is rocky from its center to its surface, but Europa appears to be covered with ice. The long cracks on this moon's surface may be the result of breaks in the sheet of ice floating on a liquid water layer below. Because Europa's surface has only a few impact craters on it, we know that its surface must be "young" and constantly changing. Europa, like Io, is heated by tides. But the tides are not as strong as on

28

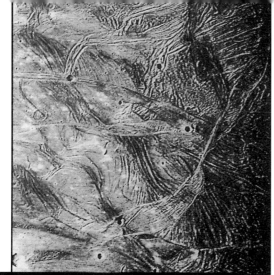

This view of Ganymede shows a close-up of "grooved" terrain, which has very few craters and must be geologically young. The area of this picture is about the size of Pennsylvania.

On Callisto, craters larger than about 100 miles in diameter do not keep their shapes as craters, since the ice cannot support the heavy rim walls. But larger impacts have occurred, as we can see in this picture. The huge impact feature, called Valhalla, has left scars more than a thousand miles away from its center, but the ridges that were formed have long since slumped, leaving a fairly level surface.

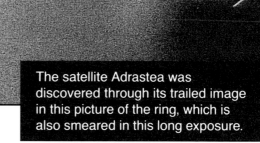

The satellite Adrastea was discovered through its trailed image in this picture of the ring, which is also smeared in this long exposure.

This satellite, named Thebe, was discovered from its shadow on the lit face of Jupiter. It has never been seen against the dark sky.

Io. On Europa, the tidal heating is enough to melt the ice below the surface, but not enough to power volcanos.

The icy surface of Ganymede is carved by internal forces that are similar to those that cause earthquakes and make mountains on Earth. Since ice is not as strong as rock, the "mountains" on Ganymede are not very high. Still, they are similar in appearance to some of the Earth's features when seen from high above. Some of the areas have many craters, while others have very few, indicating that some parts of Ganymede are newer than others. Put another way, the forces molding the surface are probably still active.

The surface of Callisto, on the other hand, is one of the most heavily cratered surfaces in the solar system, indicating that it is a dead world. Much like our Moon, it has experienced no internal activity for billions of years. The craters on both Callisto and Ganymede have a peculiar appearance, like a drop of water splashing into a puddle. This happens because the surface ice on

29

both moons acts more like water than rock when it is struck by a crater-making meteor. But since it is ice and not water, the "splash" is frozen in place!

You may be wondering what the difference is between a moon, a satellite, and a planet. If the Jovian satellites Ganymede and Callisto are the size of the planet Mercury and larger than the planet Pluto, why are they moons? Scientists use the term **planet** to mean a body orbiting the Sun, and **satellite** to mean a body orbiting around a planet (so far, we have not found any satellites of satellites!). Note that **Moon** is the formal name of Earth's satellite. Satellites of the other planets should not, properly speaking, be called "moons," but we do commonly use the term "moon" for the satellites of other planets.

Jupiter's ring is best seen when lit from behind. So, while Voyager 2 was passing through the shadow of Jupiter, directly opposite the Sun, its cameras were commanded to look back and take pictures of the ring, resulting in this mosaic of photos.

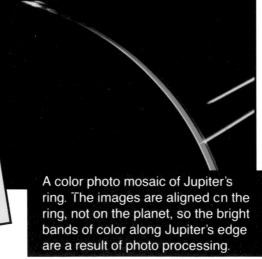

A color photo mosaic of Jupiter's ring. The images are aligned cn the ring, not on the planet, so the bright bands of color along Jupiter's edge are a result of photo processing.

RINGS AND SMALL SATELLITES

Another major discovery from Voyager 1 came as the spacecraft passed over the equator of Jupiter. Just two years earlier, in 1977, scientists on Earth had discovered rings around the planet Uranus, so the Voyager scientists were eager to see whether Jupiter might also have a faint ring that was not visible from the Earth. The cameras were

7/9/79 *Jupiter CA*, 4:21 p.m ., 403,120 miles (650,200 km) above surface

commanded to take two very-long-exposure pictures just as the spacecraft passed over the equator. One picture didn't come out, but the other — a blurred, overexposed image — showed the presence of a ring.

Now that the scientists knew there was indeed a Jovian ring, they were able to do much better with Voyager 2 four months later. Voyager 2 discovered that Jupiter's ring is unlike those of either Saturn or Uranus—it is "thin," in the sense that it is wispy. You can mostly just see right through it, as you can with a rainbow. In fact, you can hardly see it unless the conditions of lighting are just right—in this case, when the ring particles are viewed from behind.

While photographing the ring, Voyager 2 discovered a satellite, now named Adrastea (ad-rah-STEE-uh), orbiting Jupiter just at the outer edge of the ring. After months of carefully examining pictures taken by both Voyagers 1 and 2, Steve Synnott of JPL discovered two other satellites, now named Metis (MEE-tis) and Thebe (THEE-bee). These two tiny moons were discovered

Amalthea is a dark, reddish, potato-shaped satellite about 170 miles long and 100 miles wide.

in an interesting way: their silhouettes, or shadows, were seen cast against the lit face of Jupiter. Scientists believe that Jupiter's ring is actually a cloud of dust that has been splashed off Metis and Adrastea and perhaps other smaller satellites by the meteors that continually strike them.

Amalthea (am-ul-THEE-uh), the innermost satellite known before the Voyagers' arrival, is an elongated, rocky body. It is very red, like Io, but unlike the Galilean satellites it is also very dark. Thus, its surface must be made of a different material than any of the Galilean satellites.

PLANET WATCH: SHARING THE WORK

One of the great advantages of the Voyager mission was that there were two spacecraft, so the work load could be divided. Each spacecraft could focus on certain targets, depending on its sister ship to take care of the other ones.

Thus, at Jupiter, Voyager 1 came closest to the satellites Io and Callisto, while Voyager 2 came closest to Europa and Ganymede. At Saturn, Voyager 1 came closest to the satellites Titan (TYT-un), Rhea (REE-uh), Dione (dy-OH-nee), and Mimas (MY-mus), while Voyager 2 came closest to Enceladus (en-SEL-uh-dus), Tethys (TEE-thus), Hyperion (hy-PEER-ee-un), and Iapetus (eye-AP-uh-tus).

A second advantage of having two spacecraft was that the experiments conducted by Voyager 2 at Jupiter and Saturn could be improved based on what had been discovered there by Voyager 1. So, after Voyager 1 discovered volcanos on Io and a ring around Jupiter, Voyager 2's cameras were targeted to take pictures of the new discoveries when it flew by Jupiter. The same was done at Saturn.

For the visits to Uranus and Neptune by Voyager 2, the engineers back on Earth were developing new computer programs so that the spacecraft could take more pictures. They had to test the programs out on the spacecraft. But because they were afraid the new routines might accidentally break some part of Voyager 2, they ran the tests on Voyager 1, which had already encountered Saturn and would not be encountering any other planets. Once the engineers were satisfied the new programs worked, they relayed them out to Voyager 2 for use at Uranus and Neptune.

The two Voyagers thus worked together, helping each other like the partners they were.

HIGHLIGHTS OF THE ENCOUNTER WITH JUPITER

- Detailed measurements of cloud motions on Jupiter
- Auroras on Jupiter
- Lightning storms in the atmosphere
- A thin ring around Jupiter
- Three more small satellites close to Jupiter discovered
- Active volcanos on Io
- Detailed pictures of the surfaces of the four large satellites

A DIFFERENT LOOK AT THE JOVIAN SYSTEM

	Model Diameter	Model Distance (from center of Jupiter)
Jupiter	beach ball 5 feet across	—
Ring	1/4 inch wide	4 feet
Metis	speck of dust	4 feet
Adrastea	speck of dust	4 feet
Amalthea	salmon egg	5 feet
Thebe	grain of sand	7 feet
Io	golf ball	13 feet
Europa	Ping-Pong ball	20 feet
Ganymede	billiard ball	35 feet
Callisto	billiard ball	62 feet
Leda	speck of dust	200 yards
Himalia	pin head	200 yards
Lysithea	speck of dust	200 yards
Elara	grain of sand	200 yards
Ananke	speck of dust	400 yards
Carme	speck of dust	400 yards
Pasiphae	grain of sand	400 yards
Sinope	speck of dust	400 yards

1
2   7/10/79 *Emerges from behind Jupiter, 4:20 p.m., regains radio contact*

3

SATURN
THE SECOND STOP ON THE TOUR

The second stop for the two Voyager spacecraft on their tour of the outer solar system was at the ringed planet Saturn, two years after the Jupiter flybys. Saturn is smaller than Jupiter, but similar to it in many ways. It is a giant ball of gas, mostly hydrogen and helium, with a small core of rock and ice. Saturn has lots of medium-sized and smaller moons, each very different from one another. Unlike Jupiter, Saturn has only one large moon, Titan. Most important to the Voyager scientists were Saturn's beautiful rings, which have fascinated astronomers for centuries. The rings are believed to be the fragments of one or more moons that broke up close to the planet long ago but that remain trapped in orbit by the planet's powerful gravity.

Voyager 1 came closest to Saturn on November 12, 1980. It flew within about 77,000 miles (125,000 km) of the planet and took more than 13,500 pictures. Because it was now so far away from Earth, the spacecraft's radio signals were much weaker when they were received. It was necessary for Voyager to send its pictures much more slowly so that they would be received correctly by the antennas on Earth. Still, Voyager 1 sent data to Earth at a rate of 45,000 bits per second!

DAY 1,163   ▮ 11/11/80   *Titan CA (closest approach),* 11:06 p.m., 2,480 miles (4,000 km)

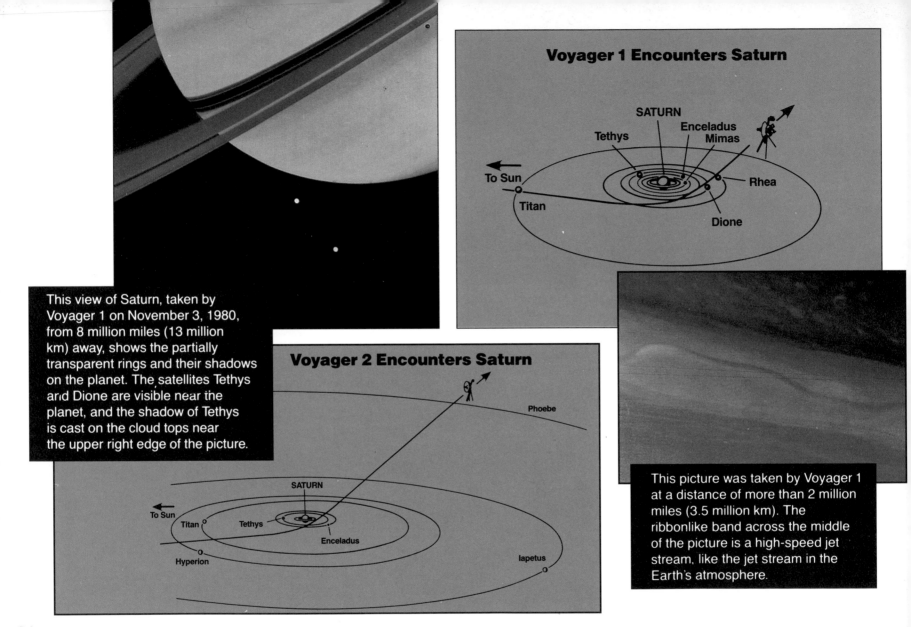

Voyager 1 Encounters Saturn

SATURN

Tethys

Enceladus
Mimas

To Sun

Titan

Rhea

Dione

This view of Saturn, taken by Voyager 1 on November 3, 1980, from 8 million miles (13 million km) away, shows the partially transparent rings and their shadows on the planet. The satellites Tethys and Dione are visible near the planet, and the shadow of Tethys is cast on the cloud tops near the upper right edge of the picture.

Voyager 2 Encounters Saturn

Phoebe

SATURN

To Sun

Titan   Tethys

Enceladus

Hyperion

Iapetus

This picture was taken by Voyager 1 at a distance of more than 2 million miles (3.5 million km). The ribbonlike band across the middle of the picture is a high-speed jet stream, like the jet stream in the Earth's atmosphere.

34

Voyager 2 took this picture of Saturn on August 4, 1981, from a distance of 13 million miles (21 million km). Three satellites are visible below the planet: Tethys, Dione, and Rhea (from left to right). The shadow of Tethys is visible on the disk of Saturn.

11/11/80 *Emerges from behind Titan,* 11:22 p.m., regains radio contact

Saturn is almost twice as far from the Sun as Jupiter; it is nine and a half AUs from the Sun. Its year (the time it takes to go around the Sun) is almost 30 Earth years long. Like Jupiter, Saturn spins very quickly, taking just over 10 hours to rotate once.

As Voyager 1 swept toward Saturn in November 1980, each day brought new details about the planet, the rings, and the moons. Measurements of winds in Saturn's atmosphere showed that they are the strongest anywhere in the solar system, with speeds of up to 900 miles per hour. Some of the smaller satellites showed evidence of very large impacts that had created huge craters and had almost split the satellites into pieces. Indeed, this appears to have been the fate of closer satellites, which are now the rings.

Perhaps the most exciting discovery was that Saturn's three main rings, which are visible from Earth, turned out to be made up of thousands of ringlets, each with varying patterns of thickness and composition.

Voyager 2 followed its sister ship and passed Saturn on August 25, 1981. It flew even closer, to about 62,500 miles (100,000 km) from the planet. It took 11,850 pictures while its other instruments all clicked away, carefully measuring many aspects of the Saturnian system.

THE RINGS OF SATURN

The rings of Saturn are a beautiful sight, even when seen from the Earth through a small telescope. But the Voyagers revealed wonders undreamed of by earthly astronomers. As mentioned earlier, the "three" rings we see from Earth turned out to be composed of thousands of little ringlets. At close range, these ringlets looked like the grooves on a phonograph record. Most of the features in the rings are just thicker and thinner parts, but there are true gaps in some places, caused by small satellites orbiting within the rings or just beyond them. The gravity of these satellites forces ring particles out of their paths. A single satellite within a broad ring clears a gap in the ring. Two satellites in nearby orbits can squeeze ring matter between them into a narrow, stringlike ring. Such satellites have been nicknamed **shepherds.**

The gravity of nearby satellites also makes waves in the rings, like boat wakes. By studying these waves, scientists have been able to determine how much matter is in the rings. It turns out that if all the ring material were gathered together into one ball, it would be the size of one of Saturn's smaller moons—for example, Mimas.

Saturn's rings are very flat and thin. If you made a model of Saturn and its rings with a ball and a sheet of paper the thickness of this page, the planet would have to be 200 feet across and the rings 500 feet across for you to get an accurate picture of the thinness of the rings in comparison to their width.

How Were the Rings Formed?

We see craters on the smaller satellites that were caused by collisions with comets or giant meteors. These collisions were so powerful that they nearly blew the satellites apart. It is likely that in the past some of these moons were struck by even larger things that *did* blow them apart. The blown-up bits made a temporary ring around Saturn in the orbit path of the former satellite. Normally, most of the pieces of a shattered moon gather back together in a few months, and the satellite becomes whole again. But if the satellite was very close to Saturn, the force of gravity from the planet could have prevented the satellite pieces from sticking back together, so the ring would have remained a ring. Over millions of years, such a ring of debris can spread out, becoming broad rings.

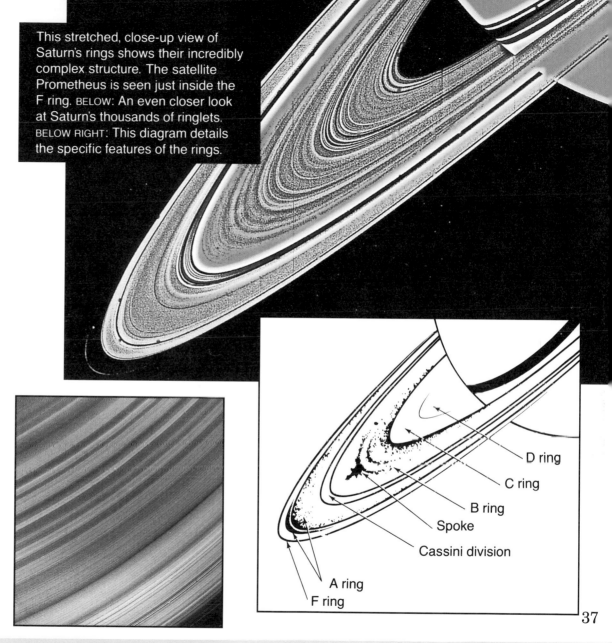

This stretched, close-up view of Saturn's rings shows their incredibly complex structure. The satellite Prometheus is seen just inside the F ring. BELOW: An even closer look at Saturn's thousands of ringlets. BELOW RIGHT: This diagram details the specific features of the rings.

D ring
C ring
B ring
Spoke
Cassini division
A ring
F ring

37

■ 11/12/80 *Mimas CA, 7:05 p.m.,*
54,830 miles (88,440 km)

■ 11/12/80 *Passes behind Saturn,*
7:08 p.m., loses radio contact

■ 11/12/80 *Enceladus CA, 7:15 p.m.,*
125,240 miles (202,000 km)

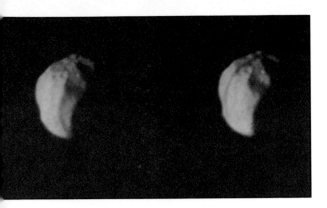

Two images of Epimetheus, taken 13 minutes apart. A comparison of the photos shows that the shadow of one of the rings is moving slowly across the face of the satellite.

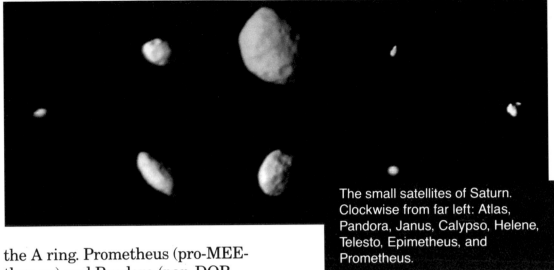

The small satellites of Saturn. Clockwise from far left: Atlas, Pandora, Janus, Calypso, Helene, Telesto, Epimetheus, and Prometheus.

THE PLANET WITH THE MOST SATELLITES

Saturn has more known satellites than any other planet. Before the Voyager flybys, nine moons had been observed and their orbits measured. Two others had been glimpsed, but their orbits were uncertain. Voyager 1 discovered three more moons, all very close to the rings. Atlas, the closest moon, is just outside the main rings and helps to confine the outer edge of

the A ring. Prometheus (pro-MEE-thee-us) and Pandora (pan-DOR-uh), the "F-ring shepherds," are next and are on either side of this narrow ring. Epimetheus (ep-uh-MEE-thee-us) and Janus (JAY-nus), which had been glimpsed in 1966 and were again observed from the Earth only a short time before the Voyagers arrived, share the same orbit. Every few years, one of these two moons tries to pass the other, but their gravity fields cause them to "bounce" off each other without actually touching (sort of like two magnets that repel each other without touching). All of these satellites are very small and are probably fragments of the one or

more larger satellites that broke up to form the rings.

The next four major satellites are somewhat larger. Mimas shows no obvious sign of geologic activity, but it has a crater so large that whatever struck it must have nearly shattered it. Scientists believe that it may have been broken up by even larger collisions and then been reassembled from a temporary ring. The next satellite out, Enceladus, has almost no craters on large parts of it, suggesting that there has been "recent" geologic activity. However, unlike Jupiter's Io, we do not see currently active volcanos on

38

1

■ **11/12/80** *Emerges from behind Saturn, 8:40 p.m., regains radio contact* ■ **11/12/80** *Emerges from behind rings, 9:04 p.m.*

2

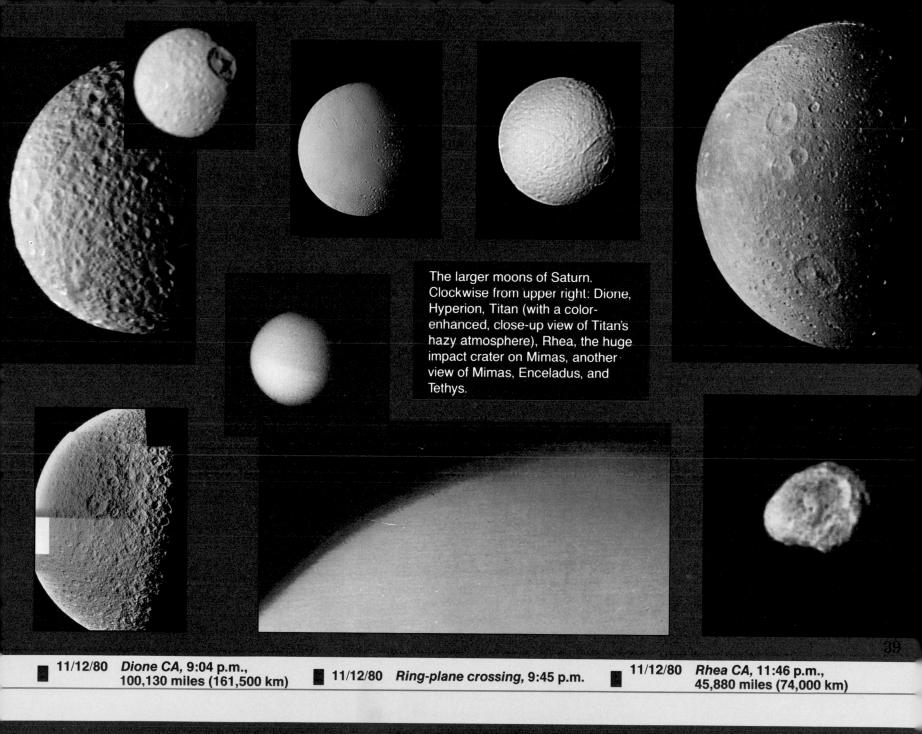

The larger moons of Saturn. Clockwise from upper right: Dione, Hyperion, Titan (with a color-enhanced, close-up view of Titan's hazy atmosphere), Rhea, the huge impact crater on Mimas, another view of Mimas, Enceladus, and Tethys.

11/12/80 *Dione CA, 9:04 p.m.,*
100,130 miles (161,500 km)

11/12/80 *Ring-plane crossing, 9:45 p.m.*

11/12/80 *Rhea CA, 11:46 p.m.,*
45,880 miles (74,000 km)

Enceladus. Tethys and Dione also show some signs of geologic activity, but these features are heavily covered by craters, indicating that the surfaces have not changed for most of the age of the satellites.

Enceladus and Dione are in orbital resonance, like Jupiter's Io and Europa. That is, Enceladus makes two trips around Saturn for every one of Dione's. Thus, these two satellites also experience tidal heating, like Io and Europa. Because they are smaller, though, the heating is not so great. Still, the heating is enough to cause occasional geologic activity.

The next major satellite out, still larger, is Rhea. It is covered with impact craters, and Voyager 1 could see no evidence of past geologic activity. Rhea and all of the other Saturnian satellites we have talked about so far appear to be made of almost pure ice and, like the rings, are very bright.

One of Voyager 1's most important targets was the planet's large satellite, Titan. The Voyager scientists were thrilled to discover that unlike any other moon in the solar system, Titan had its own

The F ring was first discovered by Pioneer 11 in 1979. It was thought that this ring was confined by shepherd satellites, and this picture is a dramatic confirmation of that theory. The photo was a lucky one, since the two shepherd moons — Prometheus and Pandora — pass each other only about every 25 days.

dense atmosphere (even denser than the Earth's), made mostly of nitrogen. But they were also disappointed to find that the clouds in Titan's atmosphere were so thick that the surface below was completely invisible. Measurements from Voyager 1 showed that the surface was very cold, almost −300°F. Some astronomers think that Titan's surface might have

oceans made of liquid methane. But this is one mystery that neither Voyager could solve.

Just beyond Titan is another very small moon, Hyperion. Although it is not much smaller than Mimas or Enceladus, Hyperion is unlike these and the other satellites in that its shape is flattened and irregular, so that it looks somewhat like a hamburger. The force of the tide from Saturn causes it to tumble with an irregular spin.

The outermost satellite of Saturn is Phoebe. Neither Voyager got close enough to get a very good picture of this very dark body. Scientists think Saturn probably captured this asteroid or cometlike fragment into its gravitational field long ago.

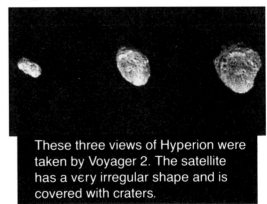

These three views of Hyperion were taken by Voyager 2. The satellite has a very irregular shape and is covered with craters.

40

A VERY STRANGE MOON: IAPETUS

One of the strangest objects in the entire solar system is Saturn's moon Iapetus. This satellite is black as coal on one side and white as snow on the other. No other known satellite anywhere in the solar system shows such an extreme variation in brightness from one side to the other.

Voyager's photographs show that the white side of Iapetus is similar to the bright, icy moon Rhea. This makes sense, because the density of Iapetus indicates that, like the inner satellites of Saturn, it is made mostly of ice. But how did the other side come to be black? Even with close-up pictures like the one here, the Voyager scientists are unable to decide. Perhaps the black material rained down onto its surface from the small, dark satellite Phoebe, orbiting beyond Iapetus. Or perhaps this material bubbled out of the interior of Iapetus. The mystery may not be solved until 2002, when the Cassini spacecraft visits Saturn and takes even more detailed pictures. Stay tuned!

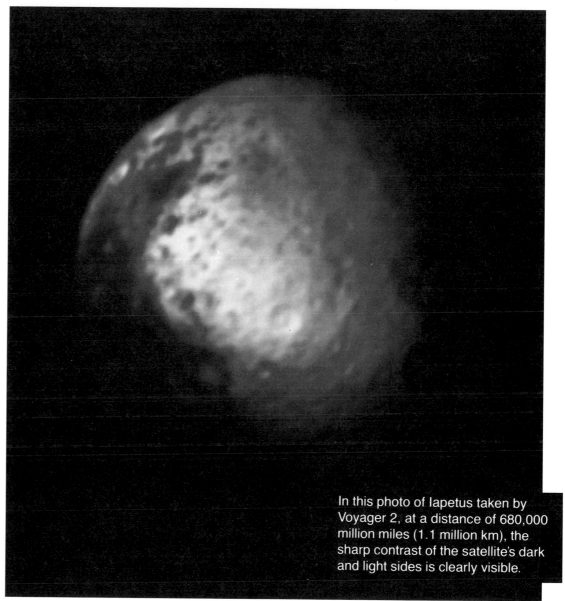

In this photo of Iapetus taken by Voyager 2, at a distance of 680,000 million miles (1.1 million km), the sharp contrast of the satellite's dark and light sides is clearly visible.

8/25/81 *Titan CA*, 1:00 a.m., 412,900 miles (665,960 km)   8/25/81 *Saturn CA*, 9:51 p.m., 62,500 miles (100,800 km)

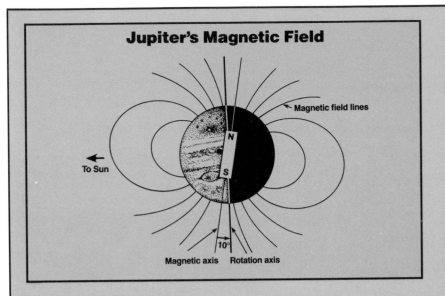

Jupiter's Magnetic Field

Magnetic field lines

To Sun

10°

Magnetic axis   Rotation axis

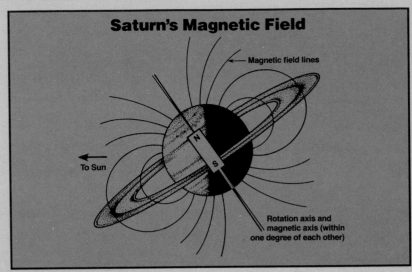

Saturn's Magnetic Field

Magnetic field lines

To Sun

Rotation axis and magnetic axis (within one degree of each other)

PLANET WATCH: MAGNETIC FIELDS AND RADIATION BELTS

Most of the planets are surrounded by invisible **magnetic fields.** These fields are believed to arise from electric currents flowing within the metal cores of each planet. Just as a magnet has north and south poles, the magnetic fields around the planets also have north and south poles.

The Earth's magnetic field is nearly lined up with its rotation axis (the axis about which the planet spins). This is why the needle of a compass points nearly north from anywhere. Jupiter and Saturn also have magnetic fields that are nearly lined up with their rotation axes. Like the Earth, their fields appear to come from near the centers, or cores, of the planets. The magnetic fields of Uranus and Neptune are tilted far from the directions of their spin axes (60° for Uranus, 47° for Neptune). Moreover, the fields are not centered in the planets. On Neptune, the field is so far off center that it is more than

10 times stronger on some parts of the planet's surface than on others. Although scientists are not sure why the fields are offset from the centers of the planets, they do know that it means both planets have electrically conducting (metallic) layers at least as far from their centers as the offsets of the fields.

The magnetic fields surrounding the planets trap particles from the solar wind (the stream of charged particles flowing out from the Sun). The trapped particles form what is called a **radiation belt** around each planet. The radiation belt

1
2

■ 8/25/81 *Enceladus CA, 10:12 p.m.,* 54,030 miles (87,140 km) (data lost)   ■ 8/25/81 *Passes behind Saturn, 10:26 p.m., loses radio contact*

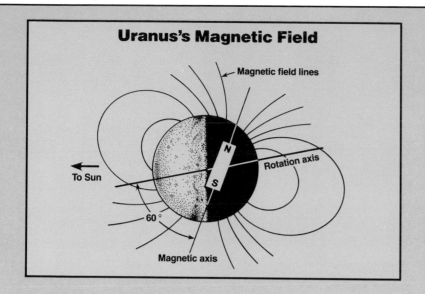

Uranus's Magnetic Field

Magnetic field lines

N

S

To Sun

Rotation axis

60°

Magnetic axis

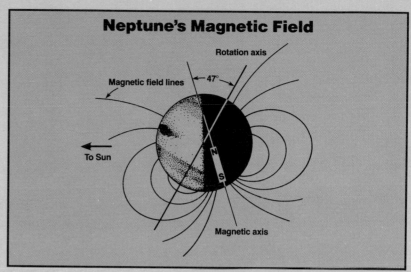

Neptune's Magnetic Field

Rotation axis

47°

Magnetic field lines

N

S

To Sun

Magnetic axis

surrounding the Earth—called the Van Allen radiation belt—causes the auroras (the northern and southern lights) near the poles. Similar belts around the four giant planets also cause auroras, which were seen by the Voyagers. Because the magnetic fields are so tilted on Uranus and Neptune, the auroras occur closer to the equators than to the poles on these planets.

The Voyagers carried instruments to measure the radiation as they flew through the radiation belt of each planet. At Jupiter, the radiation was so strong that it

almost disabled the spacecraft's cameras and computers. Saturn's magnetic field is almost as strong as Jupiter's, but its radiation belt is much weaker. The reason for this is that the rings, which are located just about where the most intense radiation belt would be, absorb the particles from the solar wind as soon as they arrive. Satellites also absorb the radiation, and some satellites have been "seen" by the gaps they cause in the radiation belts.

After their visits to Saturn, the two Voyager spacecraft followed

very different paths. Voyager 1's path through the Saturnian system had been carefully chosen so it could come close to both the rings and the large satellite Titan. As a result, Saturn's gravity flung Voyager 1 high up out of the plane of the solar system. Once Voyager 1 left the plane, it could never again meet another planet but would simply continue on into outer space.

Voyager 2's path was different. Saturn's gravity was carefully used to target the spacecraft toward the next planet out: Uranus.

43

HIGHLIGHTS OF THE ENCOUNTER WITH SATURN

- Wind speeds of up to 900 miles per hour, the fastest in the solar system
- Main rings look like thousands of ringlets, appearing like the grooves on a record
- Co-orbital and shepherd satellites in and near the rings
- Detailed measurements of Titan's atmospheric structure
- Geologic activity on Enceladus, possibly ice volcanism
- "Hamburger" shape of Hyperion
- Light and dark sides of Iapetus photographed, but not understood

A DIFFERENT LOOK AT THE SATURNIAN SYSTEM

	Model Diameter	Model Distance (from center of Saturn)
Saturn	beach ball, 4 feet across	
B ring, outer edge	10 inches wide	4.0 feet
A ring, outer edge	6 inches wide	4.49 feet
Atlas	speck of dust	4.52 feet
Prometheus	grain of sand	4.57 feet
F ring	string	4.60 feet
Pandora	grain of sand	4.65 feet
Epimetheus	grain of sand	5.0 feet
Janus	pin head	5.0 feet
Mimas	pea	6.0 feet
Enceladus	pea	7.8 feet
Tethys	marble	10 feet
Telesto	speck of dust	10 feet
Calypso	speck of dust	10 feet
Dione	marble	12 feet
Helene	speck of dust	12 feet
Rhea	marble	17 feet
Titan	billiard ball	40 feet
Hyperion	pea	50 feet
Iapetus	marble	50 yards
Phoebe	pin head	200 yards

URANUS

4

ENCOUNTER WITH THE TILTED PLANET

After its encounter with Saturn, Voyager 2 was living on borrowed time. Remember, the spacecraft was designed to go only to Jupiter and Saturn. Although the JPL scientists and engineers knew that there was a chance to encounter the next two planets further out, Uranus and Neptune, they were not certain that the spacecraft would work that long or so distant from the Sun. It took Voyager 2 four years to get to Saturn. It would take another four and a half years to get to Uranus and three and a half years more to get to Neptune. Could the spacecraft make it?

The early signs were not good. In just the first year of the mission, one of Voyager 2's radio receivers had failed completely, and the second receiver was working improperly. Furthermore, just as Voyager 2 passed Saturn, the scan platform carrying the cameras got stuck — it wouldn't move! The engineers on Earth had to analyze these problems by studying the data sent back by Voyager 2, which was now more than a billion miles away. They had to figure out how to fix the problems, and then send commands to teach the spacecraft how to fix itself. Fortunately for us, the engineers succeeded, and Voyager 2 sailed on to its rendezvous with Uranus.

Fortunately, too, there were some positive developments during the long journey to the spacecraft's next encounter. The engineers thought of new ways to run Voyager 2 more

45

efficiently. They also sent "smarter" programs to its computers. Perhaps most important, they figured out a way for the spacecraft to hold itself more steady while taking pictures in the faint sunlight. The engineers also taught Voyager how to code the pictures so that they could be transmitted more efficiently back home.

This picture of Uranus is processed as the eye would see it (above), and with color differences exaggerated (opposite) to bring out the banded patterns in the atmosphere. Uranus's pole is at the center of the dark area, pointing nearly toward the Sun.

If you were to make a model of Uranus using a beach ball two feet in diameter, the ring system would be four to five feet in diameter, and all but one of the nine rings would be thinner than a human hair! Imagine how hard it would be to see a strand of hair around a beach ball. Now imagine that the hair is black, and the sunlight is 400 times fainter than the sunlight we see on Earth. It's amazing that Voyager 2 saw anything at all!

Uranus, which is twice as far from the Sun as Saturn, takes 84 Earth years to complete one "year." In spite of its great distance, we did know quite a bit about Uranus before the Voyager 2 encounter. We knew that it is much smaller than Jupiter and Saturn, although it is still about four times the size of Earth. We knew that it weighs about 14 times as much as Earth. Uranus contains less hydrogen and helium than Jupiter and Saturn. Instead, its atmosphere is made up of water, ammonia, and methane. But, like Jupiter and Saturn, it has a core of ice and rock that is about the size of the Earth.

The strangest thing we knew about Uranus is that it is tilted so that it is on its side. Earth's rotation axis is tilted about 23°, and this causes the different seasons here. The other planets are similar. But Uranus is tilted more than 98°, so that its north pole points almost directly at the Sun at one point in its orbit, and the south pole points almost directly at the Sun half an orbit (42 Earth years) later.

Scientists did not know how this odd tilt would affect the weather on

46

The **average density** (weight compared to size) of a body is the most fundamental clue scientists have to the composition of a planet or satellite. Suppose you had three balls, all the same size: a Ping-Pong ball, a solid rubber ball, and a solid metal ball. No matter how similar the balls might appear on the outside, you could quickly tell them apart by their different weights. We can do the same with planets and satellites: we can "weigh" them by measuring how strongly their fields of gravity act on one another or on a spacecraft flying nearby. The planet Mercury is so heavy that we know it must be about half iron. Venus, Earth, Mars, Io, and Europa are mostly rock, with smaller amounts of iron and/or "ice" (we use the term "ice" to mean not only water ice, but also compounds of carbon, nitrogen, oxygen, and hydrogen, and not necessarily in solid form). From their densities, scientists can tell that Uranus and Neptune, along with most of their satellites, Jupiter's satellites Ganymede and Callisto, and most of the satellites of Saturn, have little rock or metal in them and must be made mostly of ice. Jupiter and Saturn are even less dense than ice and must be mostly hydrogen and helium gases, with smaller amounts of ice and rock.

Voyager 2 took 5,800 pictures of Uranus as it came within 51,000 miles (81,440 km) of the planet's cloud tops on January 24, 1986. The spacecraft sent data to Earth at a rate of 21,600 bits per second.

47

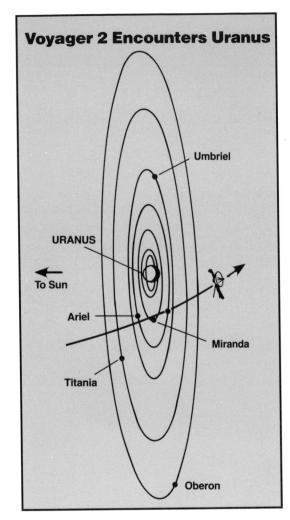

Voyager 2 Encounters Uranus

Umbriel

URANUS

← To Sun

Ariel

Miranda

Titania

Oberon

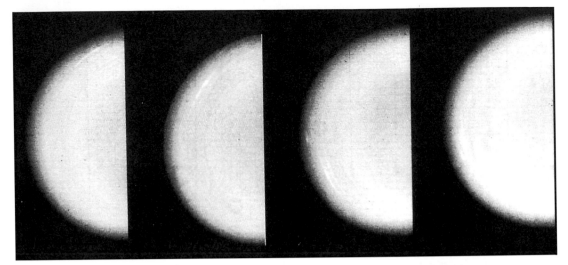

This time-lapse sequence (over a 4½-hour period) shows the counterclockwise rotation of the Uranian atmosphere.

Uranus. They thought that perhaps there would be even bigger storms on Uranus than on Jupiter and Saturn. But instead, Voyager 2 found a planet that was almost totally featureless. As it grew closer and closer to Uranus, all Voyager could see was a greenish-blue ball, with almost no visible features. The color came from methane gas in the upper atmosphere, which scattered the sunlight and hid the details of the clouds below.

Using very intense computer processing, the scientists could eventually see some features of the clouds, and from these they could determine that the planet rotates once in about 17 hours. But little else could be learned about the planet's deep atmosphere. Meanwhile, the other instruments on Voyager 2 were busy studying the magnetic field and the radiation belts, the planet's faint rings, and its five large satellites.

RINGS OF A DIFFERENT KIND

Only six months before the Voyagers were launched in 1977, astronomers measured the brightness of a star that was passing behind Uranus. (When an object in space passes behind

48

another object, the event is called an **occultation**.) They hoped to probe the planet's atmosphere in this way. They were surprised to see the star "wink out" six times before it passed behind the planet and six more times afterward. This revealed to them that Uranus is encircled by a system of thin, stringlike rings (a total of nine rings were confirmed by further observations). All of the rings are extremely narrow.

When Voyager 2 reached Uranus in January 1986, it discovered a tenth narrow ring, as well as one very broad ring about 1,600 miles (2,500 km) wide. This broad ring is inside all the other rings.

The remarkable thing about Voyager 2's observations of the rings of Uranus is that the instruments on board were not designed to see them. By the time the rings were discovered, the Voyagers had already been built — and, anyway, the original plan did not include going on to Uranus. To get the pictures of the rings and satellites that we see here, JPL engineers had to actually reprogram the spacecraft. They had to give it abilities no one thought possible when it was built and launched, and they had to do so when Voyager was already more than a billion miles from Earth.

SATELLITES OF URANUS

Scientists expected to find shepherd satellites keeping the ring particles confined in narrow rings, and maybe others between the rings and the innermost known moon, Miranda (mih-RAN-duh). They were rewarded with more new discoveries than at any other planet, ten new moons found in all! The two shepherd satellites discovered confining the Epsilon ring were named Cordelia (cor-DEEL-yuh) and Ophelia (oh-FEEL-yuh). The other eight are outside the ring system and are very small, like the tiny satellites discovered around Jupiter. Probably made of the same material as the rings, these moons orbit far enough from Uranus that they were able to gather together into satellites rather than remaining rings of dust. The outermost of the new satellites discovered — Puck — is by far the

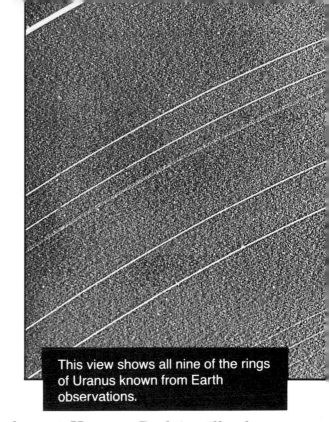

This view shows all nine of the rings of Uranus known from Earth observations.

largest. However, Puck is still only one-third the size of Miranda, which was the smallest moon known before the encounter. It is also inside the orbit of Miranda.

Five larger satellites — Miranda, Ariel (AR-ee-el), Umbriel (UM-bree-el), Titania (ty-TAY-nee-uh), and Oberon (OH-buh-ron) — were known before Voyager 2 arrived at Uranus in January 1986. They

49

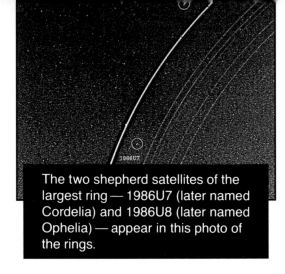

The two shepherd satellites of the largest ring — 1986U7 (later named Cordelia) and 1986U8 (later named Ophelia) — appear in this photo of the rings.

Miranda is the innermost of the larger Uranian satellites. Some of the surfaces are very young, with very few impact craters.

The surface of Ariel also reveals evidence of much geologic activity, including flow features similar to the lava flows on the Earth.

are similar in size to the larger icy satellites of Saturn (excluding Titan) and range from 340 miles to 1,970 miles in diameter. They also have similar densities to the Saturnian moons, indicating that they, too, are made up mostly of ice. But a surprising difference is that the moons of Uranus have fairly dark surfaces. The darkest surfaces seem to be the oldest. Why are the Uranian moons — and rings, too — so dark? Scientists suspect that over time, the satellites and rings may have been covered by a dark material that forms when methane is exposed to sunlight. (The darkened methane is not unlike a

substance familiar here on Earth: smog from car exhaust!) The oldest surfaces should have the thickest coats and appear the darkest. The tiny satellites and the rings are the darkest of all. Does this mean they are the oldest? No one knows for sure. They may just be made of rock or some other material, rather than ice.

By far the most unusual of the moons of Uranus is Miranda, which has huge fields that look like recent lava flows. These fields have far fewer craters than do other areas of Miranda, so they appear to be young. But at this distance from the Sun, water ice is too cold to

melt into a kind of "water lava." Thus, scientists are not sure what compound makes up the lava on Miranda. One possibility is ammonia.

Three of the other four large satellites are similar to Miranda, although perhaps less dramatic. The farther each is from Uranus, the less activity it shows. Because these moons are larger than Miranda and have stronger fields of gravity, the features are squeezed flatter to their surfaces. Only Umbriel is remarkably different, with a surface that is little altered by geologic activity and that is much darker than the others. No one knows why.

50

Umbriel is strikingly unlike the other satellites. It is much darker and shows very little evidence of recent geologic activity. Only a couple of bright patches are visible in this view.

Titania appears to be a near twin of Ariel, with similar flow features. There are more craters, though, so the surface is older and less altered.

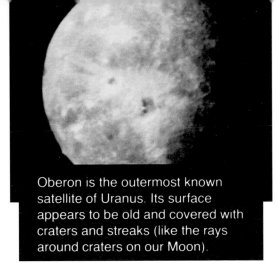

Oberon is the outermost known satellite of Uranus. Its surface appears to be old and covered with craters and streaks (like the rays around craters on our Moon).

PLANET WATCH: OCCULTATION OBSERVATIONS

Remember how scientists accidentally discovered rings around Uranus when they were measuring the brightness of a star as it passed behind the planet? Because the star seemed to "wink out" several times, the scientists realized that something—the rings—was blocking the starlight.

Since that time, astronomers have used this method, called occultation, to map out the Uranian rings in great detail, to look for rings around Neptune, and even to measure the size and shapes of asteroids. To understand how this works, imagine that you are out in the country on a dark night and can see the light from a farmhouse far away across a field. As you walk along the road, the light blinks out and then reappears. Even though you cannot see it, you known there must be a tree, a pole, or something else out in the field blocking the light. If you were to move back and forth and up and down, you would be able to see the outline of the object.

Even though it was not possible to add instruments to the Voyagers in the six months between the discovery of the Uranian rings and the launches, scientists quickly realized that a suitable occultation instrument was already aboard. The instrument, called a photopolarimeter, was intended mainly to measure the brightness of light from planetary atmospheres, satellite surfaces, and the rings. At the time the instrument was designed, no one thought to use it to probe rings.

PLANET WATCH *continued*

Although the photopolarimeter on Voyager 1 broke even before it got to Jupiter, the instrument on Voyager 2 worked for all four encounters. In addition to the measurements it was designed to make, the photopolarimeter was used to probe the rings of Saturn and Uranus. Details as small as 100 feet across could be seen in the occultation profiles. From these detailed profiles, scientists discovered the wakes in the narrow rings and gaps that revealed the presence of unseen shepherd satellites.

HIGHLIGHTS OF THE ENCOUNTER WITH URANUS

- **One new narrow ring and one broad, but very thin, ring discovered**
- **Ten new satellites discovered, including shepherd moons around the thickest ring**
- **The satellite Miranda showed evidence of extensive geologic activity**

A DIFFERENT LOOK AT THE URANIAN SYSTEM

	Model Diameter	Model Distance (from center of Uranus)
Uranus	beach ball 20 inches across	
1986U2R ring	a 1-inch-wide ribbon	16.0 inches
Ring 6	strand of hair	16.5 inches
Ring 5	strand of hair	16.6 inches
Ring 4	strand of hair	16.8 inches
Alpha ring	thread	17.6 inches
Beta ring	thread	18.0 inches
Eta ring	strand of hair	18.6 inches
Gamma ring	strand of hair	18.8 inches
Delta ring	strand of hair	19.0 inches
Cordelia	speck of dust	19.6 inches
1986U1R ring	strand of hair	19.7 inches
Epsilon ring	string	20.1 inches
Ophelia	speck of dust	21.2 inches
Bianca	speck of dust	23.3 inches
Cressida	grain of sand	24.3 inches
Desdemona	grain of sand	24.7 inches
Juliet	grain of sand	25.4 inches
Portia	grain of sand	26.0 inches
Rosalind	grain of sand	27.5 inches
Belinda	grain of sand	29.6 inches
Puck	pin head	33.9 inches
Miranda	salmon egg	4 feet
Ariel	marble	6 feet
Umbriel	marble	9 feet
Titania	marble	14 feet
Oberon	marble	19 feet

5

NEPTUNE
THE LAST GREAT ENCOUNTER

The final stop on Voyager's tour of the outer solar system was the beautiful blue planet Neptune, a full 30 AUs from the Sun. Neptune is so far away that it takes 164 Earth years for it to go around the Sun once. In fact, Neptune has not even completed one of its years since it was discovered in 1846!

What we knew about Neptune before the Voyager 2 encounter led scientists to suspect that it was similar to Uranus. We knew it is slightly smaller than Uranus (a little less than four times the size of the Earth), but slightly heavier, too (about 17 times heavier than Earth). Scientists suspected that Neptune's rotation time was similar to that of Uranus — about 17 hours — but they knew with certainty that its axis is not as tilted. The most fascinating things known about Neptune before the encounter had to do with its satellite and rings. A large satellite — Triton (TRYT-un) — was known, which circled the planet in

Voyager 2 flew closer to Neptune than it had to any other planet. It passed over Neptune's north pole only 3,000 miles above the cloud tops — an amazing achievement, given that the spacecraft had traveled for 12 years and more than 5 *billion* miles (8 billion km) to get there! The spacecraft sent data to Earth at a rate of 21,600 bits per second.

53

DAY 4,387 ■ 8/25/89 *Inbound ring-plane crossing, 12:09 a.m., 9,610 miles (15,500 km) outside brightest ring*

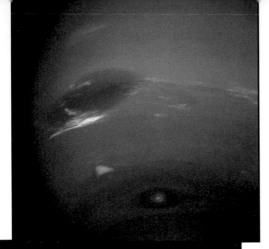

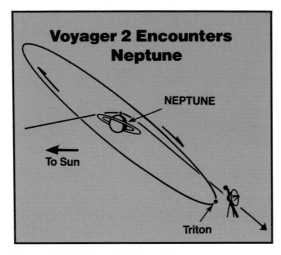

Voyager 2 Encounters Neptune

NEPTUNE

To Sun

Triton

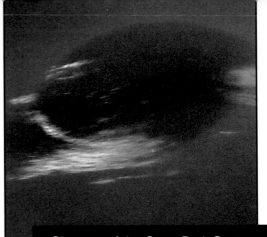

This picture was taken a few days after the picture on the right page. Notice how the clouds have moved relative to one another. The bright cloud below the Great Dark Spot (about halfway between it and the other dark spot) is the feature named Scooter.

Close-up of the Great Dark Spot, taken from 1.7 million miles (2.8 million km) away. The Great Dark Spot is about the size of the Earth, and the smallest features visible in this picture are about 30 miles (50 km) across. The bright clouds surrounding the dark spot are higher-altitude cirrus clouds, much like the high-altitude clouds that lie above storm clouds in the Earth's atmosphere.

a **retrograde**, or backward, orbit (that is, clockwise when looked at from Neptune's north pole rather than counterclockwise). Also, it was thought that Neptune might have rings. Partial rings, or arcs, had been discovered orbiting the planet. Thus, scientists were hoping the Neptune encounter would bring interesting discoveries—and it did.

When close-up pictures of Neptune reached Earth on August 25, 1989, we saw a beautiful blue ball with wonderfully detailed white clouds. The biggest feature was a giant storm, almost as big as Earth. The Voyager scientists were very excited, because they had seen something like this before. Neptune's Great Dark Spot, as they called it, looked very much like Jupiter's Great Red Spot. Was it possible that, like the Great Red Spot, the huge dark storm on Neptune had been raging for countless years? There was no way of knowing, but the feature did mean that the weather patterns on Neptune were probably much the same as the weather patterns on Jupiter.

A second, smaller feature was also discovered, near Neptune's south pole. The feature consists of an ever-changing pattern of white clouds. Because that feature moves very rapidly around the planet, the JPL scientists named it Scooter. Like the Great Dark Spot, Scooter behaves much like some of the storms on Jupiter.

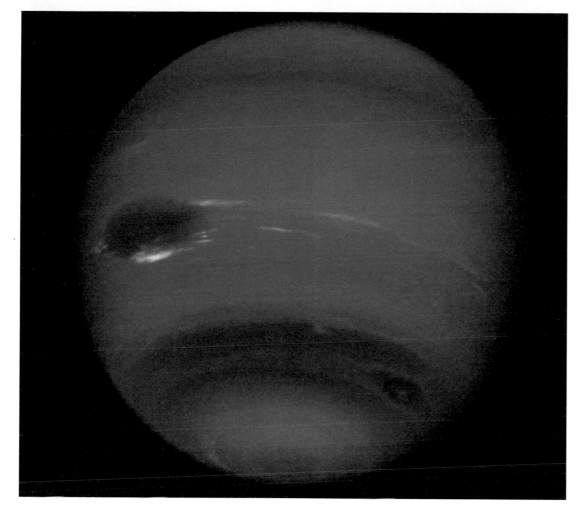

These clouds are in a jet stream, looking very much like similar clouds above the Earth as seen from a jetliner. You can see the shadows of the clouds on the smooth cloud layer about 30 miles (50 km) below them.

View of the whole disk of Neptune, taken a week before the encounter, at a distance of about 5 million miles (8 million km).

But differences were also found between the two planets. One difference is their color. Neptune's beautiful blue comes from methane gas (just like the methane gas on Uranus), while Jupiter's red color comes from ammonia and complex hydrocarbon gases. Another remarkable difference is that the winds on Neptune blow from east to west, which is the opposite direction of the winds on Uranus and Saturn, as well as most of the winds on Jupiter.

55

A view of the rings lit from behind. The crescent of Neptune is nearly lost in the glare to the lower right.

RINGS AND NEW SATELLITES

Following the discovery of rings around Uranus in 1977 and the Voyager 1 discovery in 1979 of a ring around Jupiter, scientists tried very hard to find rings around Neptune. Each time Neptune passed over or near a star as seen from Earth, they eagerly watched for telltale winks of the star's light before and after the star passed behind the planet.

Several of these occultation events yielded nothing. Then, on May 24, 1981, two University of Arizona astronomers, Harold Reitsema and William Hubbard, observed an occultation of something at least 50 miles across near Neptune. The trouble was, nothing was seen on the other side of the planet, so whatever they were observing couldn't be an encircling ring. By the time Voyager 2 arrived at Neptune eight years later, five more reliable observations had been made. But, as with the first one, there were no matching objects on the other side of the planet. The

only explanation scientists could come up with was that Neptune might be surrounded by long, thin "arcs" — incomplete rings that extended only partway around the planet.

As Voyager 2 sped closer to the blue planet, scientists were eager to uncover evidence of the ring arcs. Eight weeks before the closest encounter, a new satellite was discovered close to Neptune. As weeks passed, more satellites were found, some of them orbiting very near to where the scientists suspected the ring arcs were. Finally, two weeks before the closest encounter, a ring arc was detected. But it wasn't until after the spacecraft had passed Neptune and was "looking" back toward the backlit planet that complete rings became clearly visible.

We now know that Neptune has three fairly distinct, narrow rings and one broad ring circling it. Two of the narrow rings and the broad ring are too thin to block enough starlight to show up as occultations. The third, outermost narrow ring is also too thin to block starlight, except for three thicker segments—

56

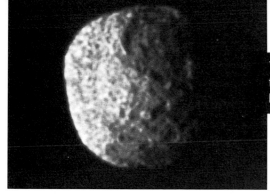

This is the best picture of 1989N1, the largest of the moons discovered by Voyager 2. The impact that made the big crater faintly visible probably almost split the satellite apart.

the ring arcs. The even thinner, broad sheet of dust extends from halfway between the outer two rings to perhaps as far as the planet.

Once Voyager 2 had revealed the location of the rings and the orbit period of the arcs, scientists could calculate where the arcs were at the time of the occultations that had been seen over the past decade. Five of the six events lined up with the dense arc segments, in distance from the planet as well as position in orbit. But what about the sixth event, which happened to be the first and biggest occultation of them all? Miraculously, it matched up with the position of 1989N1, the largest of the new satellites discovered. The chance of seeing an occultation by such a small satellite was only a few in a thousand — but it happened!

PLANET WATCH: COMPARING THE GIANT PLANETS

What did the Voyagers find on their long journey of exploration through the outer solar system? They discovered that each planet was very different from its neighbors. Before Voyager, scientists had thought that Jupiter and Saturn were fairly similar, and that Uranus and Neptune made another similar pair. But Voyager showed that each of these four planets has its own unique identity.

Jupiter has the most active atmosphere, with its complex and ever-changing cloud patterns. Saturn's atmosphere looks milder, but in fact the winds were far stronger than the winds on Jupiter. Uranus is so bland that we could hardly make out any clouds at all. And Neptune is similar to Jupiter, though less complex, and the winds there blow in the opposite direction.

Jupiter has one thin ring, nearly invisible from Earth. Saturn has a beautiful system of rings that Voyager showed is made up of thousands of ringlets. Uranus has many faint rings, but like Jupiter's ring, they are almost impossible to see from Earth. Finally, Neptune has a number of faint rings, with clumpy structures spread through one of them.

Voyager also taught us to expect the unexpected. At each planet, the scientists guessed that the satellites would be covered with craters, like the Earth's Moon. Some satellites were, but others — such as Io and Triton — showed signs of tremendous activity. Voyager showed us that even far away from the Sun, where it was bitterly cold, energy from sources such as tides could warm the satellites and make them active.

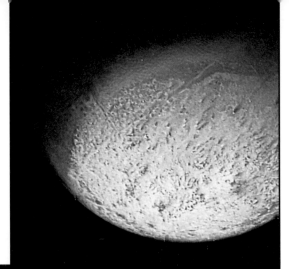

This color picture of Triton was taken by Voyager 2 from 330.000 miles (530.000 km) away. about 12 hours before its closest approach to the satellite.

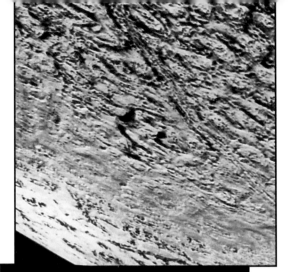

Close-up of the "cantaloupe" terrain.

TRITON: GEYSERS AND ICE LAVA

Before the Voyager 2 encounter of Neptune, only two satellites were known. One, called Nereid (NEER-ee-id), is small and circles Neptune in a distant orbit, taking a full Earth year to circle the planet. The other satellite, Triton, was certain to be large, since it appears so bright in telescopes on Earth. If its surface was as bright as snow, it would still be larger than any of the Uranian satellites, and if its surface was dark, it would have to be even larger than Saturn's Titan, one of the largest satellites in the solar system. Scientists believed it might have a dense atmosphere (like that of Titan) and oceans of liquid nitrogen. The strangest thing we knew about Triton before Voyager 2 arrived was that, as mentioned earlier, its orbit around Neptune is backward. Most of the satellites in the solar system circle their planets from west to east, but Triton circles

Neptune in the opposite direction. Triton's orbit is also tipped further away from Neptune's equator than the orbit of any other large satellite around a planet in our solar system. Scientists were not sure what to make of these puzzles, so they were eager to see what Voyager would reveal.

A week or two before the encounter, scientists were able to measure the size of Triton. They discovered that it was smaller than expected—too small, in fact, to have a dense atmosphere or an ocean of any kind. But as Voyager 2 drew closer, Triton was revealed to be an exciting world nonetheless, in unexpected ways. The north polar cap appeared to be covered with frost, and several dark streaks seemed to be "painted" on top of the frost. By carefully analyzing all the pictures of Triton, scientists were able to determine that several of these streaks were venting gas and dust, like the volcanos on Io. These vents are probably more like geysers than volcanos, but they prove that Triton is geologically active.

Farther out from this pole are large areas of heavily cratered

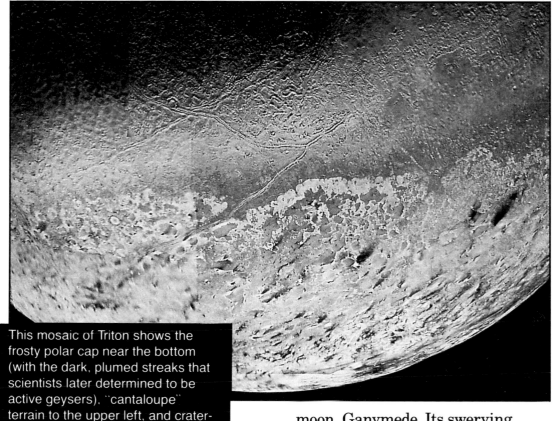

This mosaic of Triton shows the frosty polar cap near the bottom (with the dark, plumed streaks that scientists later determined to be active geysers), "cantaloupe" terrain to the upper left, and crater-covered terrain to the upper right.

terrain, probably very old and not very active. Another kind of area has been described as "cantaloupe" terrain. This area has almost no craters, so it must be younger. In some ways, the cantaloupe terrain resembles parts of Jupiter's largest moon, Ganymede. Its swerving, riverlike features are probably flows of ice "lava" that have been wrinkled and twisted by younger flows that push them about. Finally, there are large, smooth plains that are probably even younger. These areas appear to have been flooded by ice lava, but they haven't been altered by craters or drifting ice.

A note on names: The names of astronomical bodies are proposed by their discoverers (with the exception of comets, which are named after their discoverers). The proposed names are approved by the International Astronomical Union (IAU), which meets every three years. In the meantime, new discoveries are given temporary names — 1989N1, for example, which means the first satellite of Neptune discovered in 1989. Before a name is assigned, the discovery of the astronomical body must be confirmed. The IAU last met in August 1988; at that time, the Uranian satellites received their permanent names. The next meeting will be in August 1991, at which time the newly discovered Neptunian satellites will likely receive their names.

8/25/89 *Passes behind Triton, 6:49 a.m., loses radio contact*

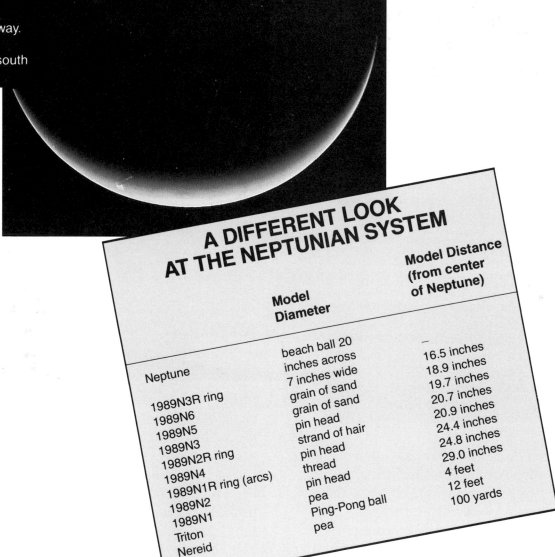

HIGHLIGHTS OF THE ENCOUNTER WITH NEPTUNE

- **Very high wind speeds, up to 300 mph, blowing the "wrong" way (east to west)**
- **Great Dark Spot, almost identical to Jupiter's Great Red Spot and at about the same latitude on the planet**
- **Three narrow rings and one broad, but thin, ring; the outermost ring has three thicker arcs within it**
- **Six new satellites discovered close to the planet**
- **Surface of the satellite Triton is geologically active, with venting ice "geysers"**

A DIFFERENT LOOK AT THE NEPTUNIAN SYSTEM

	Model Diameter	Model Distance (from center of Neptune)
Neptune	beach ball 20 inches across	
1989N3R ring	7 inches wide	16.5 inches
1989N6	grain of sand	18.9 inches
1989N5	grain of sand	19.7 inches
1989N3	pin head	20.7 inches
1989N2R ring	strand of hair	20.9 inches
1989N4	pin head	24.4 inches
1989N1R ring (arcs)	thread	24.8 inches
1989N2	pin head	29.0 inches
1989N1	pea	4 feet
Triton	Ping-Pong ball	12 feet
Nereid	pea	100 yards

1

2 ■ **8/25/89 *Emerges from behind Triton, 6:43 a.m., regains radio contact***

INTERSTELLAR SPACE

THE VOYAGER MISSION CONTINUES

6

When Voyager 2 crossed the orbit of Neptune in August 1989, it had traveled a distance of almost 5 billion miles in the 12 years since it was launched from Earth. It was moving away from the Sun at a speed of 36,900 miles per hour. Ahead of it there were no more planets to encounter (since Pluto was in a different part of the solar system), only the infinite depths of interstellar space.

But Voyager 2's job was not over yet. Voyager 2 and its sister ship, Voyager 1, are to this day still exploring new regions of space. The ultraviolet spectrometer on board each spacecraft looks at stars and galaxies, and instruments continue to measure the magnetic field and charged particles coming from the Sun. Both spacecraft periodically radio their information back to Earth. The Voyagers are still on the job!

One of the most important tasks for the two spacecraft is to look for the boundary between our solar system and the rest of the galaxy. This boundary, called the **heliopause**, is the place where the stream of charged particles flowing out from the Sun (the solar wind) becomes so weak that it is overcome

8/90   *Voyager 2 crosses the orbit of Pluto.*

by the stronger flow of charged particles between the stars. When the Voyagers cross the heliopause, they will no longer be part of our solar system. They will become true interstellar spacecraft.

Where exactly is the heliopause? No one knows for certain. Scientists once thought it might be fairly close, perhaps just beyond the orbit of Jupiter. But they now suspect that it is much farther away, perhaps 50 to 150 times the Earth's distance from the Sun.

As of 1985, two other spacecraft—Pioneer 10 and Pioneer 11—were ahead of the Voyagers in the journey toward the heliopause. But since the Voyagers are traveling faster, they have already passed Pioneer 11, and in a few decades they will also be farther from the Sun than Pioneer 10. Not bad, considering that Pioneer 10 had a five-year head start!

How long can the Voyagers continue to operate? There is enough fuel for the small control rockets on board to keep the antenna on each spacecraft pointed toward Earth for the next 40 to 50 years. The radios transmit signals that are strong enough to be received on Earth until the year 2037. But the real limit involves the RTGs. The radioactive plutonium that supplies the heat for the electricity that runs all the instruments on board is decaying, and as it gets older it is able to make less and less electricity. As the amount of electricity drops, the engineers will be forced to turn off some of the scientific instruments. By the year 2000, there will be too little electricity to move the scan platform holding the cameras and spectrometers. In 2009, there will no longer be enough power to keep all the particles and fields instruments turned on at the same time. Finally, somewhere around 2016 for Voyager 1 and 2018 for Voyager 2, there will no longer be enough power to run any of the instruments. At that point, the engineers will likely send each Voyager a message to turn itself off.

The Voyagers, of course, will continue to move outward along their paths through interstellar space. Along the way they will pass through the **Oort cloud**, a vast field of comets that surrounds our solar system. Comets are primitive, icy bodies that we believe date back to the origin of the solar system. The Oort cloud contains an estimated 5 trillion comets. But outer space is so big that it is unlikely that either Voyager will come close to any of the comets!

Beyond the Oort cloud, the Voyagers will travel between the stars. The engineers have carefully calculated the paths of each spacecraft for the next 1 million years. Because stars are extremely far apart, neither Voyager will come close to any of them.

THE VOYAGER MESSAGE

Perhaps someday an interstellar traveler will find one of the Voyagers. If that happens, the traveler will find a special gift on each spacecraft. That gift is a golden record that contains greetings from the people of Earth and tells a little about our planet.

The Voyager records look like ordinary phonograph records. But instead of being made of plastic,

1 ■ 2000 *Voyager 1, now 76.3 AUs from the Sun, no longer has enough power to run its scan platform.*

2 ■ 2000 *Now 59.7 AUs from the Sun, Voyager 2 no longer has enough power to run its scan platform.*

2016   *Voyager 1 no longer has enough power to run any of its scientific instruments.*

they are made of copper and coated with gold. The gold coating will protect them from decay in outer space. Each record is also protected by a cover, and on the cover are pictures that explain how to play it. Also packed with each record is the needle for the record player.

Carefully recorded on the records are messages. One is from Kurt Waldheim, who was the secretary general of the United Nations in 1977. Another is from Jimmy Carter, the president of the United States in 1977. Others are greetings from children around the world, recorded in many different languages. There are also selections of music on the record, including classical, jazz, and even rock and roll.

Each Voyager record also carries 116 photographs, carefully coded and recorded. There are pictures of a newborn baby, of an astronaut, and of people going about their daily business. There are pictures of cities and of landscapes. Some pictures show human beings, just as in a medical textbook, to show other beings what our bodies are like.

A traveler who finds one of the Voyagers will learn a great deal about us, both from the record and pictures and from the spacecraft itself. The spacecraft will reveal our level of technology at the time it was built. It will also show that we chose to use that technology to peacefully explore outer space.

Each Voyager is like a bottle with a note inside it, thrown into the cosmic ocean. Perhaps in a few million years it will wash up on some interstellar shore, and some other beings out there will know that they are not alone in the galaxy. Perhaps they'll even find their way to Earth to learn more about the creators of Voyager.

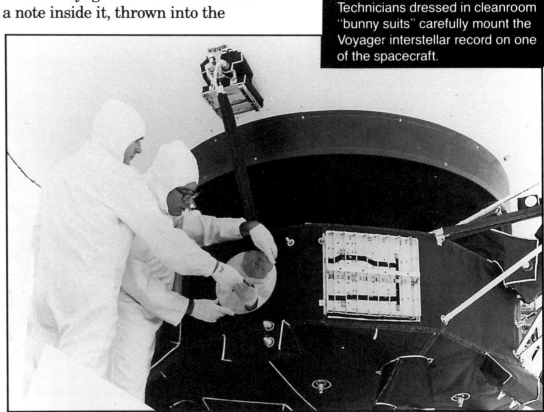

Technicians dressed in cleanroom "bunny suits" carefully mount the Voyager interstellar record on one of the spacecraft.

7

FUTURE MISSIONS

FURTHER ADVENTURES IN OUTER SPACE

The Voyager mission was a great adventure of exploration. It revealed many new worlds and showed us just how fascinating a place our solar system is. But Voyager was just one step in the exploration of outer space. Just as Voyager followed a path first blazed by Pioneers 10 and 11, new spacecraft will now follow where Voyager 1 and Voyager 2 have been. Still other spacecraft will explore entirely new places. All these spacecraft will communicate with scientists on Earth the same way the Voyagers do—through the Deep Space Network.

MOVING TO JUPITER: GALILEO

The first spacecraft to follow Voyager is called **Galileo**. Named for the scientist who discovered the largest moons of Jupiter, Galileo is in many ways similar to Voyager, with a large radio antenna and RTGs. But Galileo's job is to go into orbit around Jupiter and stay there for many years, studying the planet and its four large satellites in detail. We can think of Voyager 1 and Voyager 2 as tourists that just visited the Jovian system for a few days. But Galileo is moving to

65

5/4/89   *Magellan launched to Venus.*

10/18/89   *Galileo spacecraft launched to Jupiter, via Venus and Earth gravity-assist encounters.*

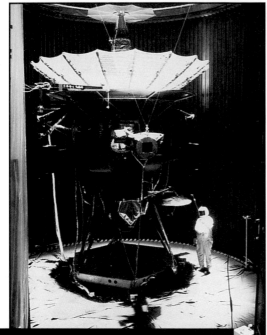

The Galileo spacecraft undergoes testing in the thermal vacuum chamber at JPL where conditions in outer space can be accurately simulated. Note how large the spacecraft is compared to the technician standing next to it.

The Galileo spacecraft launch, October 18, 1989. The large white cylinder under the spacecraft is the rocket that sent it out of Earth orbit toward Venus.

Photo courtesy of IMAX.

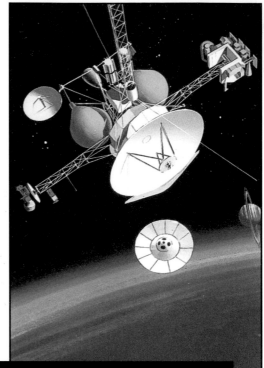

An artist's painting of the Cassini spacecraft as it will appear in orbit around Saturn, releasing its atmospheric entry probe toward the cloud-covered satellite Titan.

Jupiter to stay, and it is expected to send detailed scientific measurements back to Earth for many years.

Galileo, which was launched from the space shuttle *Atlantis* in October 1989, is too heavy to have been sent directly to Jupiter by the space shuttle. Instead, it will use gravity assists from Venus and the Earth to gain enough energy for its trip. Galileo flew by Venus in February 1990 and sent back new pictures and measurements of that cloud-covered planet. It is scheduled to fly by the Earth twice, in December 1990 and then in December 1992. After the first flyby, it will soar outward about halfway to Jupiter before returning. The second flyby will give it enough energy to go all

■ **2/9/90** *Galileo encounters Venus.*

■ **4/24/90** *Hubble Space Telescope launched into Earth orbit.*

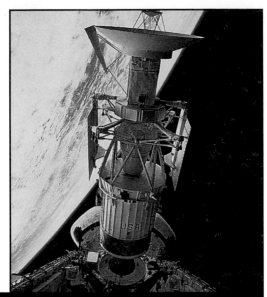

Magellan is launched from the space shuttle *Atlantis* on May 4, 1990.

The CRAF spacecraft as it may appear when it meets with comet Kopff, planned for the year 2000, and releases a penetrator to land on the comet nucleus.

The Mars Observer spacecraft is scheduled to be launched on a Titan III rocket in 1992 and placed in orbit around Mars.

When CRAF encounters comet Kopff, scientists expect it will look like Halley's comet, as seen in this 1986 photo taken by the Giotto spacecraft.

A cut-away drawing of the CRAF penetrator as it may appear when planted in the surface of a comet. There it will make key scientific measurements and radio them back to the CRAF orbiter.

■ **8/10/90** *Magellan arrives at Venus.*   ■ **12/8/90** *Galileo scheduled to fly by the Earth*

■ **10/90** *Ulysses scheduled to be launched*

the way to Jupiter. On the way, it will be the first spacecraft to fly close to an asteroid (the asteroid belt lies between the orbits of Mars and Jupiter).

Galileo is scheduled to reach Jupiter in December 1995. It is carrying a probe to drop into Jupiter's dense atmosphere. The measurements from the probe will be radioed back to Galileo, and then to Earth. Meanwhile, the Galileo spacecraft will orbit Jupiter for at least two years, or longer if the spacecraft remains healthy. With each orbit, it will closely observe one of the big satellites. Each satellite encounter will be carefully planned so that the flyby will slightly alter Galileo's orbit, putting it on a new course toward its encounter with another satellite.

One suggestion for a future mission to Mars is a rover vehicle that will drive around and pick up rocks, placing them aboard a rocket that will be sent back to Earth so the rocks can be analyzed.

RETURN TO SATURN: CASSINI

Another mission being readied to follow Voyager is called **Cassini**. Cassini is named for the seventeenth-century astronomer who was one of the first people

to study Saturn and its rings (remember the Cassini division?). The Cassini mission will place a spacecraft in orbit around Saturn to study the planet, its rings, and its satellites for many years.

Cassini also will carry a probe, which will be used to study the

The Cassini mission is being designed and built jointly by the United States and the European Space Agency. It is scheduled to be launched on a Titan IV rocket in 1996 and arrive at Saturn in 2002. Along the way it, too, will fly by a large asteroid, and then it will pass close to Jupiter. Like both Voyagers, Cassini will use Jupiter's gravity to help it get to Saturn.

68

Scheduled to be launched from the space shuttle in October 1990, the Ulysses spacecraft will use Jupiter's gravity to fling it into an orbit over the north and south poles of the Sun.

dense clouds of the big satellite Titan. As the probe descends to the surface of Titan on a parachute, it will take measurements and send them to Earth. On board the Cassini spacecraft will be a radar instrument that will be able to peer through the clouds of Titan and take pictures of the moon's surface, something that the Voyagers could not do.

An interesting feature of both the Galileo and Magellan missions is that they both use spare parts left over from the building of the Voyager spacecraft. The radio antenna on Magellan is a Voyager spare, and Galileo uses leftover radio transmitters. By using spare parts, the engineers were able to build the spacecraft for less money.

VISITOR TO VENUS: MAGELLAN

Another spacecraft has already arrived at its destination. Launched in 1989, **Magellan** arrived at Venus in August 1990 and is now orbiting the planet, using radar to take pictures of the Venusian surface beneath the dense cloud layer. The radar pictures will allow scientists to make maps of the surface of Venus, something that could never be done with ordinary cameras. Magellan will transmit data to Earth for nine months.

TAILING A COMET: CRAF

An important future mission is called **Comet Rendezvous/ Asteroid Flyby**, or **CRAF**. The CRAF spacecraft is very similar to Cassini, but it will orbit a comet, not a planet. CRAF will not only study the comet from a very low orbit (about 40 miles), but it will also drop a load of instruments— collectively called a penetrator— onto the comet's surface. The CRAF spacecraft will follow the comet as it orbits the Sun, collecting comet dust and gas and analyzing them on board in miniature scientific laboratories. At one point, CRAF will even fly down the comet's tail for 30,000 miles.

CRAF is scheduled to be launched on a Titan IV rocket in 1995 and to match orbits with the comet in the year 2000. Like Cassini, it will encounter an asteroid. And like Galileo, both CRAF and Cassini need to fly by the Earth, using it for a gravity assist to help them reach their destinations.

■ 12/8/92 *Galileo scheduled to fly by the Earth for the second time*

■ 8/92 *Mars Observer scheduled to be launched*

The Hubble Space Telescope being deployed from the space shuttle *Discovery* on April 25, 1990. The large brown patch is a solar cell panel used to generate electricity.

OTHER MISSIONS TO EXPLORE OUTER SPACE

Many other spacecraft missions are now under construction or in the early planning stages. One such mission is **Mars Observer,** a spacecraft that is scheduled to be launched on a Titan III rocket in 1992. Mars Observer will orbit around Mars and study it for one full Martian year (1.88 Earth years). It will map the planet's surface and study its atmosphere, just as the Landsat spacecraft have studied the Earth's atmosphere.

An even more ambitious project now under consideration is **Mars Rover and Sample Return.** This mission will land a self-propelled rover vehicle on Mars. Scientists on Earth will drive the rover by remote control, exploring the Martian surface just as if they were there themselves. The rover will also collect rock and soil samples and load them into a rocket that will carry them back to Earth. The samples will then be analyzed by scientists. It is hoped the rocks and soil will reveal something about the complex history of Mars, just as rocks returned from the Moon told us so much about its history.

As we study the planets, we sometimes forget that the biggest object in the solar system is the Sun. A new spacecraft to study the Sun, called **Ulysses,** is scheduled to be launched on the space shuttle in October 1990. Ulysses is on a unique trajectory that will use a Jupiter gravity assist to fling it into an orbit high above the plane of the solar system and over the north and south poles of the Sun. The Sun's poles are not easily visible from Earth, and Ulysses will likely provide the first close look at the Sun from this unique viewpoint.

Some of the most important new missions involve powerful new telescopes that will be put in orbit around the Earth. The Earth's atmosphere prevents telescopes on the ground from having a clear view of outer space. Telescopes in orbit will not only have a perfect view of stars and galaxies, but they will also be able to operate around the clock since there is no day or night in outer space.

The first of these big telescopes is the **Hubble Space Telescope**, which was launched from the space shuttle *Discovery* on April 25, 1990.

Hubble's main mirror is almost eight feet (2.4 meters) in diameter, allowing the telescope to see faint galaxies billions of light-years away (a light-year is the distance a ray of

8/93 *Mars Observer scheduled to arrive at Mars*

8/93 *Galileo scheduled to encounter the asteroid Ida, at a distance of 930 miles (1,500 km)*

light travels in one year, or about 6 trillion miles; the nearest star, Alpha Centauri, is 4.3 light-years from the Sun). Early testing of the Hubble Space Telescope after launch revealed a number of unexpected technical problems, which engineers and scientists are busy trying to fix. The space shuttle is scheduled to visit Hubble in 1993 to attach new scientific instruments, and astronauts may make additional repairs at that time.

Another important telescope now being readied for launch is the **Gamma Ray Observatory**, scheduled to be launched later in 1990. Two other telescopes, the **Advanced X-Ray Astronomy Facility** and the **Space Infrared Telescope**, are currently being designed.

Each of these telescopes looks at light that is invisible to our eyes — namely, X rays and infrared light. By studying the X rays and infrared light that reach these telescopes, we can learn a great deal about what is going on in distant parts of our galaxy or other galaxies.

One of the most exciting benefits of the space program is that we can

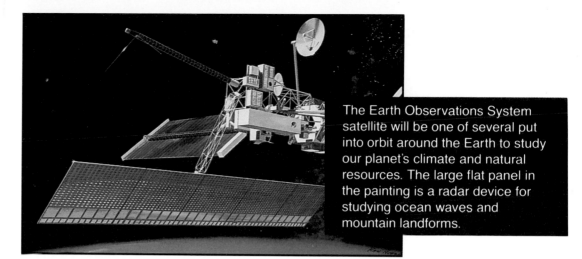

The Earth Observations System satellite will be one of several put into orbit around the Earth to study our planet's climate and natural resources. The large flat panel in the painting is a radar device for studying ocean waves and mountain landforms.

use what we learn about the other planets to understand our own Earth even better. A new series of orbiting satellites called the **Earth Observations System,** or **EOS,** will study the Earth's atmosphere and climate, natural resources, and landforms. One of the important goals of EOS is to understand how human activity can change the composition of the atmosphere and climate on Earth. With this knowledge, we can protect the environment and make the Earth a safer place to live. The EOS satellites are scheduled to be launched in the late 1990s.

Other spacecraft planned for future missions may orbit Mercury and study that planet in detail, or may orbit several asteroids in the asteroid belt. Surely one day a spacecraft will visit the tiny outermost planet, Pluto, and its one known moon, Charon. And plans are already on the drawing board for a spacecraft that will fly into the Sun.

The exploration of outer space is an ongoing adventure. Each new spacecraft makes wondrous new discoveries and tells us more and more about our solar system and universe. Voyager was a very exciting part of this adventure. One day, people may even be able to visit the places where Voyager has been. And it is Voyager that will have shown us the way.

71

SOLAR SYSTEM AND PLANETARY TABLES

THE SOLAR SYSTEM

Object	Diameter miles	km	Distance from Sun millions of miles	millions of km	Orbit Period in Earth years
Sun	820,200	1,320,000	—	—	—
Mercury	3,032	4,879	36	58	0.24
Venus	7,521	12,104	67	108	0.62
Earth	7,926	12,756	93	150	1.00
Mars	4,221	6,794	143	230	1.88
Ceres*	584	933	257	414	4.60
Jupiter	88,846	142,984	483	778	11.87
Saturn	74,898	120,536	890	1,433	29.65
Uranus	31,763	51,118	1,779	2,863	83.74
Neptune	30,770	49,520	2,807	4,518	165.95
Pluto	1,444	2,324	3,666	5,900	247.69

*This is the largest asteroid in the solar system and the first one discovered.

THE JOVIAN SYSTEM

Object	Diameter miles	km	Distance from center of Jupiter miles	km	Orbit Period in Earth days
Jupiter	88,846	142,984	—	—	—
Ring	500 (width)	800	80,000	129,000	0.298
Metis	25	40	79,510	127,960	0.2948
Adrastea	12	20	80,140	128,980	0.2983
Amalthea	170 x 100*	270 x 160*	112,650	181,300	0.4981
Thebe	60	100	137,900	221,900	0.6745
Io	2,256	3,630	262,000	421,600	1.769
Europa	1,950	3,138	416,900	670,900	3.551
Ganymede	3,270	5,262	664,900	1,070,000	7.155
Callisto	2,983	4,800	1,170,000	1,883,000	16.689
Leda	10	15	6,893,000	11,094,000	238.72
Himalia	110	180	7,133,000	11,480,000	250.57
Lysithea	25	40	7,282,000	11,720,000	259.22
Elara	50	80	7,293,000	11,737,000	259.65
Ananke	20	30	13,173,000	21,200,000	631
Carme	27	44	14,043,000	22,600,000	692
Pasiphae	43	70	14,602,000	23,500,000	735
Sinope	25	40	14,726,000	23,700,000	758

*When a satellite is not spherical, multiple figures are given to indicate the range of dimensions.

12/7/95   *Galileo scheduled to arrive at Jupiter. It will drop a probe into the Jovian atmosphere.*

THE SATURNIAN SYSTEM

Object	Diameter miles	km	Distance from center of Saturn miles	km	Orbit Period in Earth days
Saturn	74,898	120,536	—	—	—
B ring	15,800 (width)	25,500	72,950*	117,400*	0.474
A ring	9,130 (width)	14,700	84,900*	136,600*	0.595
Atlas	17 x 24**	28 x 38**	85,826	137,640	0.602
Prometheus	87 x 60 x 46**	140 x 100 x 74**	86,590	139,350	0.613
F ring	60 (width)	100	87,180	140,300	0.621
Pandora	68 x 53 x 41**	110 x 86 x 66**	88,050	141,700	0.629
Epimetheus	87 x 72 x 60**	140 x 116 x 100**	94,090	151,422	0.694
Janus	137 x 118 x 100**	220 x 190 x 160**	94,120	151,472	0.695
Mimas	245	394	115,280	185,520	0.942
Enceladus	312	502	147,900	238,020	1.370
Tethys	651	1,048	183,090	294,660	1.888
Telesto	14	23	183,090	294,660	1.888
Calypso	19 x 16 x 10**	30 x 26 x 16**	183,090	294,660	1.888
Dione	695	1,118	234,500	377,400	2.737
Helene	22 x 20 x 19**	36 x 32 x 30**	234,500	377,400	2.737
Rhea	949	1,528	327,490	527,040	4.518
Titan	3,449	5,550	759,220	1,221,850	15.945
Hyperion	217 x 149 x 124**	350 x 240 x 200**	920,310	1,481,100	21.277
Iapetus	892	1,436	2,212,900	3,561,300	79.331
Phoebe	143 x 137 x 68**	230 x 220 x 110**	8,048,000	12,952,000	550.48

*Distance to outer edge of ring.

**When a satellite is not spherical, multiple figures are given to indicate the range of dimensions.

73

THE URANIAN SYSTEM

Object	Diameter miles		km	Distance from center of Uranus miles	km	Orbit Period in Earth days
Uranus	31,763		51,118	–	–	–
1986U2R	1,600		2,500	24,700	39,500	0.237
Ring 6	1	(width)	2	26,000	41,850	0.259
Ring 5	2	(width)	3	26,250	42,240	0.262
Ring 4	2	(width)	3	26,460	42,580	0.266
Alpha ring	6	(width)	10	27,790	44,730	0.286
Beta ring	6	(width)	10	28,380	45,670	0.295
Eta ring	1	(width)	1	29,320	47,180	0.310
Gamma ring	2	(width)	3	29,600	47,630	0.314
Delta ring	3	(width)	5	30,020	48,310	0.321
Cordelia	16		26	30,880	49,700	0.335
1986U1R ring	1	(width)	1	31,090	50,040	0.338
Epsilon ring	14–58*	(width)	22–93*	31,790	51,160	0.350
Ophelia	19		30	33,430	53,800	0.376
Bianca	14		22	36,790	59,200	0.435
Cressida	39		62	83,400	61,800	0.464
Desdemona	34		54	38,960	62,700	0.474
Juliet	52		84	40,140	64,600	0.493
Portia	67		108	41,070	66,100	0.513
Rosalind	34		54	43,430	69,900	0.558
Belinda	41		66	46,800	75,300	0.624
Puck	96		154	53,400	86,000	0.762
Miranda	169		272	80,700	129,900	1.413
Ariel	719		1,158	118,600	190,900	2.520
Umbriel	726		1,169	165,300	266,000	4.144
Titania	981		1,578	271,100	436,300	8.706
Oberon	946		1,523	362,500	583,400	13.463

*This ring is elliptical and has varying width.

THE NEPTUNIAN SYSTEM

Object	Diameter miles	km	Distance from center of Neptune miles	km	Orbit Period in Earth days
Neptune	30,770	49,520	–	–	–
1989N3R ring	1,000 (width)	1,700	26,000	41,900	0.240
1989N6	34	54	30,000	48,000	0.296
1989N5	50	80	31,000	50,000	0.313
1989N3	110	180	32,600	52,500	0.333
1989N2R ring	less than 6 (width)	less than 10	33,100	53,200	0.343
1989N4	90	150	38,500	62,000	0.429
1989N1R ring (arcs)	10	15	39,100	62,900	0.441
1989N2	120	190	45,700	73,600	0.554
1989N1	250	400	73,100	117,600	1.121
Triton	1,681	2,705	220,500	354,800	5.875*
Nereid	210	340	3,425,900**	5,513,400**	360.129

*Triton has a retrograde orbit.

**This figure is an average. Nereid actually has an elliptical orbit. It comes as close as 866,000 miles to Neptune and as distant as 5,992,000 miles.

■ **3/97** *Cassini scheduled to encounter the asteroid Maja, at a distance of 2,200 miles (3,500 km)*

GLOSSARY

Asteroids   Small, rocky bodies, up to 500 miles in diameter, that orbit the Sun, mostly between the orbits of Mars and Jupiter. Asteroids are believed to be "leftovers" from the formation of the inner planets.

Astronomical unit (AU)   One astronomical unit is 93 million miles (150 million kilometers), which is the average distance from the Earth to the Sun. Astronomical units are used to measure distances of objects in space.

Comets   Small icy bodies, from one to tens of miles across, that orbit the Sun in long, elliptic (egg-shaped) orbits. Comets are believed to be "leftovers" from the formation of the giant planets. Unlike the asteroids, which for the most part do not cross the orbits of the planets, the comets were thrown away from the region where they were formed by the powerful gravities of the outer planets (like the gravity-assist trajectories of the Voyagers). Some, which nearly escaped the Sun's gravity, remain in very long orbits, spending most of their time far beyond the planets of the solar system, in what is called the Oort cloud (about 100,000 AUs from the Sun), only occasionally passing back into the solar system where we can see them.

Cosmic rays   Very-high-energy charged particles (atoms) that are believed to come from stars beyond the galaxy.

Day   The time it takes a planet to rotate once on its axis. The term "day" is also used as a measure of time equal to the length of the Earth's day (24 hours).

Deep Space Network (DSN)   The three groups of movable radio antennas, located around the world at roughly one-third intervals, that allow JPL to talk with any of its spacecraft at any time. Each group has one large antenna (230 feet in diameter) and two smaller antennas (each 112 feet in diameter). One group is located near Barstow, California; another near Canberra, Australia; and the third near Madrid, Spain.

Heliopause   The "edge of the solar system," or the place where the stream of charged particles flowing out from the Sun (the solar wind) becomes so weak that it is overcome by the stronger flow of charged particles between the stars.

JPL   The Jet Propulsion Laboratory, founded in 1936 under the name Guggenheim Aeronautical Laboratory of the California Institute of Technology (GALCIT). In 1943, its name was changed to JPL, and in 1958 it became a contractor to NASA. Since that time, it has been primarily responsible for the unmanned exploration of the planets for NASA.

Magnetic field   The force field surrounding a magnet. The field attracts other magnets or iron objects. Most planets, including the Earth, have magnetic fields, which trap particles from the solar wind.

Moon   The Earth's satellite. The term "moon" is sometimes used to mean a satellite of another planet.

NASA   The National Aeronautics and Space Administration, founded in 1958, to carry out the space program of the United States. That program includes both manned and unmanned missions to explore outer space.

Occultation   The passage of one object behind another (the word *occult* means "hidden"). The term is used to describe the event of a star passing behind a planet or ring (as observed from the Earth).

Oort cloud   See **Comets**.

Orbit   The path of an object in space that is bound by gravity to circle around another, larger body. The planets follow orbits around the Sun; satellites follow orbits around the planets.

Planet   A large body in space that orbits the Sun. The Earth is a planet.

Plutonium   A radioactive element, similar to uranium, that releases heat energy as it decays. On the Voyagers, the heat from the decay of plutonium is converted into electricity by the radioisotope thermoelectric generators.

75

Radiation belt   A band of charged particles (atoms and electrons) surrounding a planet that are trapped by the planet's magnetic field. The Earth's radiation belts are called the Van Allen belts (named after their discoverer).

Radio antenna (dish)   A bowl-shaped structure used to collect and concentrate radio signals. The giant antennas that make up the Deep Space Network on Earth are up to 230 feet across; the ones on the Voyagers are 12½ feet across.

Radioisotope thermoelectric generators (RTGs)   Power generators of the type used on the two Voyager spacecraft. The generators create heat from the radioactive element plutonium, and the heat is converted into electricity.

Radio receiver   An electronic device that detects radio signals collected by an antenna. The receiver also amplifies the signals so they can be decoded into pictures and other information. The radio receivers on the Voyagers work the same way as a television set, but they are much more sensitive.

Radio signal   Radio waves that carry encoded commands from Earth to a spacecraft and information from a spacecraft back to Earth. The radio waves are similar to those used for television and FM radio.

Radio transmitter   An electronic device that generates radio signals with messages encoded in them. The messages are sent through radio antennas from Earth to a spacecraft or from a spacecraft to Earth. The transmitters on Earth that communicate with the Voyagers have the power of about 10,000 light bulbs; each Voyager transmitter has the power of about one light bulb.

Retrograde   Refers to a planet that spins in the opposite direction to most planets, or to a satellite that orbits its planet in the opposite direction to the planet's spin. The planet Venus has a retrograde spin; the satellite Triton has a retrograde orbit.

Ring (planetary)   A collection of particles—from fine dust and frost to house-sized boulders—that orbits around a planet and forms a ring. A ring must exist close to a planet, where the tidal force from the planet keeps the ring particles from sticking together and becoming a satellite. Some rings are confined to narrow bands a mile or so across, while others are dispersed over thousands of miles. Some are "thick" in the sense that you can't see through them, while others are very "thin" and transparent. All four of the giant planets visited by the Voyagers have rings.

Rocket motor   A motor that pushes a rocket in one direction by expelling exhaust gas in the opposite direction. A true rocket carries its own fuel and does not use air. Thus, it can work in space, where there is no air to push against.

Rotation axis (also called **spin axis**)   The imaginary line through a planet or satellite about which the planet or satellite spins. The North and South poles are the ends of this line.

Satellite   A body in space that orbits a planet. The Moon is a satellite of the Earth.

Scan platform   The platform that carries all of the instruments that have to be pointed, such as cameras. The platform can be rotated so it can scan different areas of space without having to turn the whole spacecraft.

Shepherd satellite   A small satellite near the outer edge of a planetary ring. Two shepherd satellites on either side of a ring can confine the ring into a narrow band. A single shepherd within a broad ring can clear a gap in the ring.

Solar system   The Sun (which is a star) and all the planets and other matter (satellites, asteroids, comets, meteoroids, etc.) that orbit about it. The term comes from Sol, the Roman god of the Sun.

Solar wind The stream of charged particles that flows out from the Sun. The solar wind is the source of the particles that become trapped in a planet's radiation belts.

Spacecraft A vehicle that travels through space. The Voyagers are spacecraft. Most spacecraft are rocket launched. Some are deployed by the space shuttle.

Spacecraft bus The central collection of boxes holding Voyager's electronics: computers, radio transmitters and receivers, the tape recorder, power control equipment, etc.

Star A huge ball of gas, made up mostly of hydrogen and helium, which generates energy by nuclear fusion. Deep in the center of a star the temperature is over 10 million degrees, and the pressure is so great that hydrogen atoms are "fused" together into helium atoms. A typical star like our Sun is 100 times the diameter of the Earth and 300,000 times as heavy.

Year The time it takes a planet to complete one trip around the Sun in its orbit. Jupiter's year, for example, is equal to 29½ Earth years. The term "year" is also used as a measure of time equal to the length of the Earth's year (365 days).

INDEX

7/20/2001 *CRAF scheduled to fire its penetrator into the nucleus of comet Kopff*

Mars   5, 11, 12, 21
Mercury   5, 11, 12, 21, 47
Milky Way   10
Moon, Exploring the   5, 11

N

National Aeronautics and Space
  Administration   5, 6, 13, 17
Neptune   5–7, 8, 9, 11, 12, 17, 42, 47,
  53–60
  Description of   12, 42, 53–60
  Moons   56–59
  Rings   56–57

O

Oort cloud   62

P

Pioneer 10   5, 62
Pioneer 11   5, 62
Planets   12
  Alignment of   5, 6
  Density   47
  Distance from sun   12, 21, 33, 46
  Orbits around sun   6, 33, 46
  Photographs of   11–12, 22, 27, 31,
    46, 69
Pluto   12
  Moon   12

R

Radio
  Antennas   13, 15, 16, 17
  Receivers   13, 45
  Signals   9, 17, 33
  Transmitters   13, 14, 15, 24

S

Satellites. *See* Moons under each
  planet
Saturn   5, 6, 8, 11, 12, 32, 33–42,
  44–47, 59, 68
  Description of   12, 33
  Moons   33, 34, 36, 38–40
  Orbits   40
  Rings   33, 36–38, 52, 68
Scientists   8, 9, 12, 18, 41, 46, 48,
  56, 57
Solar system   5–12
Sun   10, 12, 14, 16, 21

T

Tides   27, 28, 57
Titan III rockets   18

U

Uranus   5, 6, 11, 12, 17, 30, 42, 43,
  45–52, 57, 59

Description of   12, 46
Moons   49–51
Rings   30, 48–52, 57

V

Van Allen radiation belt   42
Venus   5, 6, 11, 12, 21, 47, 66–68
Viking missions   5, 11
Volcanos   12, 26–27, 56
Voyager missions   6–9, 12, 13–27,
  28–32, 42–49, 59, 61–64
  Assembly   18
  Communications with Earth   13,
    16, 17, 20, 25
  Designing   13, 14
  Flybys of planets   21–32, 33–36, 45
  Launches   6, 18
  Photographs   16, 22, 24, 28, 30–32,
    34, 35, 36, 41, 53–54
  Rocket motors   16
  Scientific instruments   14, 16
  Testing   18
  Voyager 1   13, 18, 22, 24, 26, 27, 31–32,
    33, 34, 38, 40–41, 42, 51, 57, 62, 65
  Voyager 2   18, 24, 25, 30, 31–32, 35,
    36, 42, 45–52, 53–54, 56–58,
    61–62, 65

A FINAL LOOK

Jupiter

Saturn

Uranus

Neptune